GRAEME
CLARK

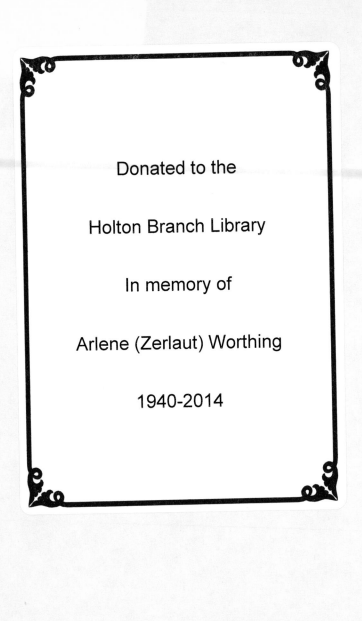

Donated to the

Holton Branch Library

In memory of

Arlene (Zerlaut) Worthing

1940-2014

GRAEME CLARK

The man who invented the bionic ear

MARK WORTHING

ALLEN&UNWIN

SYDNEY • MELBOURNE • AUCKLAND • LONDON

First published in 2015

Allen & Unwin
83 Alexander Street
Crows Nest NSW 2065
Australia
Phone: (61 2) 8425 0100
Email: info@allenandunwin.com
Web: www.allenandunwin.com

Cataloguing-in-Publication details are available
from the National Library of Australia
www.trove.nla.gov.au

ISBN 978 1 76011 315 5

Index by Puddingburn
Set in 12/17 pt Minion Pro by Post Pre-press Group, Australia
Printed and bound in Australia by Griffin Press

10 9 8 7 6 5 4 3 2 1

MIX
Paper from
responsible sources
FSC® C009448

The paper in this book is FSC® certified.
FSC® promotes environmentally responsible,
socially beneficial and economically viable
management of the world's forests.

CONTENTS

Dedicated to the memory of
Cedric Channing Worthing (1990–2013)

FOREWORD

When our oldest daughter Sophie was just 17 months old, something happened that changed our lives. We were based in Houston at the time and had the opportunity to perform as guest artists with the Australian Ballet. One day, while the company was performing in Brisbane, we were walking down a street to meet up with Mary's parents when we passed a display of balloons tied to a fence. They were colourful and caught Sophie's eye. She was excited to be able to take one. A little later, as we were walking through a corridor, the balloon popped with a loud bang. Everyone jumped. Everyone except Sophie. She just looked at us wondering why we all moved so quickly, then she looked at where her balloon had been. The expression on her face was one of bewilderment. 'Where did my balloon go?' she wondered. She had heard nothing.

We thought our daughter may have had an ear infection. We took her to be examined. When Sophie was diagnosed as profoundly deaf, it broke our hearts. To be told that she would never hear music, never speak and never hear our voices . . . Our worst fears had come true.

Sophie as a teenager with Li

My wife, Mary, decided to sacrifice her ballet career to help Sophie speak. It was just the beginning of our new journey with Sophie. We tried everything in our power to find the cause and cure, from Western medicine to Eastern treatment; nothing helped, including Sophie's hearing aids. After three long years, her progress with speech continued to be frustratingly slow.

It seemed a hopeless case until we heard about an amazing Australian invention called the cochlear implant, also known as the bionic ear. After extensive research, we realised this was our best chance for Sophie to hear and speak and be part of our hearing world—and share our love for dance and music. I still remember Sophie's eyes lighting up with excitement when she heard sound for the first time. It brought tears to our eyes. In that moment we knew that our daughter could hear. We had made the right decision.

Through our experience with Sophie's cochlear implant we came to learn a lot about the man who invented this amazing device, Professor Graeme Clark, and his research team in Melbourne. When two years later the opportunity arose for me to work professionally in Melbourne, Australia, it was not only a chance to be nearer to Mary's family, but also a chance to be closer to the centre of research into the bionic ear.

Not long after moving to Melbourne we had the opportunity to attend a fundraising event for the Bionic Ear Institute (now called the Bionics Institute) and meet Professor Clark in person. My first impressions of the man who had made this amazing device were striking. I found him to be a remarkable individual. Graeme Clark immediately impressed me as kind, gentle and extraordinarily generous of spirit. He made us feel at ease and welcome. I felt very honoured to meet the man who had given hope not only to my daughter, but to hundreds of thousands of others like her. He had given those born deaf the possibility of reaching their full potential and pursuing their dreams. Little did I suspect that I would one day serve on the board of the Bionic Ear Institute, or that my young daughter would appear with Graeme Clark and Rob Saunders, the first bionic ear recipient, on television.

When Sophie was fifteen she and Graeme Clark spoke to a group of 500 people about what it meant to have a bionic ear. She then sat down at a piano, which she had been learning since she was ten, and played a beautiful piece of music. It brought tears to the eyes of everyone present. That's what Graeme Clark's work meant for our daughter.

Sophie had a second (bilateral) cochlear implant at fourteen years of age and went on to finish school and university while continuing speech therapy. Today Sophie is fluent in both English and Auslan (Australian Sign Language) and works full time at Vicdeaf supporting the deaf and hard of hearing community in Victoria. In her spare time, Sophie volunteers at Hear For You mentoring deaf teenagers.

Li Cunxin
Artistic Director of Queensland Ballet
Author of *Mao's Last Dancer*

INTRODUCTION

An (extra)ordinary couple

I had met Professor Graeme and Margaret Clark previously on only a couple of occasions. Like most, I was in awe of Graeme's accomplishments, and struck by the graciousness he and Margaret displayed to everyone they met. When Graeme agreed to allow me to write his biography, I wasted no time beginning to gather information on his life and work. His achievements are among the best documented within Australian science, so there was no shortage of material relating to his professional life. But this was to be the story not so much of the bionic ear—that had already been told by Graeme and others—but the story of Graeme Clark. To tell *his* story I would need more than lists of accomplishments and details of scientific discoveries and surgical milestones. I needed to get some sense of the man himself.

I arranged an initial visit to the Clarks' home in Eltham, on Melbourne's eastern fringe. I was in the city for a few days for a conference, and Graeme and Margaret were able to set aside time to see me. Alongside all the stately homes in Eltham, the modest, single-storey, mud-brick home set on an acre of native scrub where Graeme and Margaret had lived for the past forty years was not what I was expecting.

Graeme comes out to greet me. He asks if I had any trouble finding the house. In fact, I had driven around gravel roads for the last twenty minutes trying to find the address.

'No,' I say. 'No problem at all.'

'Oh, good,' says Graeme. 'Some people tend to get lost coming out here.'

I am shown around the yard and house that he and Margaret had built when the oldest of their five children was only seven. I notice the remnants of an old kiln in the backyard.

'I used to turn pottery,' he says matter-of-factly. 'I found it relaxing.'

Graeme then leads me inside where Margaret had prepared biscuits and some sandwiches for a light lunch. We sit down around the kitchen table. 'Would you say grace?' Graeme asks, looking to Margaret. She says a brief prayer, then we begin to eat. The hospitality, the prayer, the simple sandwiches, the relaxed conversation: all are well-ingrained habits developed over many decades of life together.

After a short time, Margaret stands and announces, 'I'm afraid I'm going to have to excuse myself for an hour or so. I teach religious studies at the local primary school. I like to stay busy and help out still where I can. I'm sure you will have plenty to talk about with Graeme while I'm gone.'

Indeed I do. I ask about the house, the children, the pottery, Margaret's teaching—the kind of things not normally found in the published records. Graeme is relaxed and happy to reflect on the things in life that are important to him.

I am particularly interested in his family background and childhood; always a good place to start a biography. I wonder whether there are any interesting anecdotes from the family history, or any famous relatives, so I ask.

Graeme ponders a moment, then shakes his head. 'No, not really. We are a pretty ordinary family. Nothing of interest comes to mind.'

Just then Margaret returns from her teaching duties and enters the kitchen with two dresses in hand.

'I'm not sure which one to wear tomorrow,' she says to Graeme. 'These are the best two. I wish I could just go as I am.'

Graeme smiles. 'Yes, that would be nice. But I'm sure that wouldn't do. They will be expecting us to look official.'

'We are going to Canberra tomorrow,' Graeme explains. 'Prince Charles and the Duchess of Cornwall will be there and they are having some sort of reception for community leaders. The Governor-General's office think it's important we come.' Then Graeme turns his attention to the dresses. I recognise that look. He really has no idea which one is better, but is reluctant to say so. He settles for, 'I think they both look nice.'

'Well,' says Margaret, after a moment's reflection. 'I really can't wear them both.' Then she holds out the blue one. 'When we had the reception for the Queen a few years back I wore this one, and no one complained. So I suppose that would be suitable.'

'Do you think it's okay to wear the same dress for another royal meeting?' Graeme queries.

'I wouldn't think anyone would pay attention to what I'm wearing. It's not like someone will compare photographs from the last royal visit, would they?'

Margaret and Graeme both look to me as if I may somehow know the answer to this. 'I suppose,' I venture, 'there are some in the fashion world or media who just might pay attention to such things. It could be a little embarrassing to get caught out wearing the same dress eight years later. Someone might say you've only got the one fancy dress.'

'Well, I've got the two, as you can see,' adds Margaret in all seriousness.

'I guess, then,' Graeme says, 'you'd better wear the other one, just to be safe.'

Margaret seems happy with this, though still a bit bemused that anyone should care. 'I'm sorry I interrupted you two,' she says.

'That's okay,' I assure her. 'I was just asking Graeme whether there were any famous people in his family history. It might make for an interesting story or two for the book. Graeme was saying he couldn't think of any.'

Margaret pauses for a moment. 'No, no one comes to mind. We are a pretty ordinary family,' she confirms. 'Just what kind of stories are you looking for?'

'Well, anything that might be of interest to the readers. Any ancestors or relatives who would help set your family within the Australian context.'

There is silence.

'For instance,' I add, 'it would have been interesting if Graeme had some convict ancestors who had been transported to Australia.'

'Well,' Graeme says, 'two of my ancestors arrived in the First Fleet. Is that the kind of thing you are interested in?'

It is becoming clear that what might be exceptional for me is quite ordinary for the Clarks. 'Yes,' I smile. 'That is exactly the kind of thing I'm looking for.' Feeling bold, I decide to try my luck again. 'You wouldn't, perhaps, happen to have any war heroes in the family—for instance, anyone who fought at Gallipoli?'

'One of my mother's uncles fought at Gallipoli,' Graeme recalls.

'What about your mother's other uncle?' Margaret adds. 'He was a war hero.'

'Oh yes,' Graeme says to Margaret. 'He was a pilot in the Great War and received the Military Cross and two bars. And he fought at Gallipoli before that.'

'An aviator with the Military Cross,' I interject, 'is pretty impressive. I think I can mention that somewhere.'

'You really think people will want to know that kind of thing?' asks Graeme.

'They will find it very interesting,' I assure him. 'It helps to show that your story is a very Australian story. Having First Fleeters and diggers from the Great War in your ancestry is really interesting. The only other thing I could have hoped for would be a bushranger in the family tree.'

'Oh,' chuckles Graeme. 'Nothing like that in the family.' Then he pauses, before mentioning, 'My great-grandfather, however, was once held up in the goldfields by the famous bushranger Ben Hall.' Then, noting my interest, asks thoughtfully, 'That wouldn't be something you're interested in, too, would it?'

'It might be,' I smile. 'It just might be.'

Sitting in the well-used kitchen of Graeme and Margaret Clark, trying to get a measure of them, I cannot help but think: these are the most extraordinary ordinary people I've ever met.

Now I just have to understand what it was about this seemingly ordinary and unassuming man that led him to defy the scientific and medical wisdom of the day and develop the world's first functional cybernetic implant, the bionic ear.

CHAPTER 1

Tears of joy

On the morning of 1 August 1978, Graeme Clark sat down at his desk in his Eltham home overlooking the Yarra River valley. He had chosen the site soon after he and his young family arrived in Melbourne because it reminded him of the natural beauty and serenity of his childhood in Camden, New South Wales. On this particular morning he needed that serenity more than ever.

As Graeme watched the winter fog lift over the valley he took a last long look around the office where he had done so much of his thinking on the problem of how to restore hearing. He had steadied himself here when scientific colleagues in America had pronounced that a bionic ear was simply not possible, when surgical colleagues in Australia had expressed concern that his patients might die from the procedure, and when funding looked like it would run out before the project could make it to the testing stage.

His career had been dedicated almost single-mindedly to one aim—restoring hearing through a cybernetic implant, a so-called bionic ear. Today was the day he would implant the device in the first

1

human recipient. The operation would be long and complex. A dozen things could go wrong. If the patient died or the device failed, he would be unlikely to have another opportunity. It suddenly hit him that the success or failure of his entire career would be decided in the course of the next twelve hours. He paused to say a prayer for himself and his patient. Then he began the drive into the city to the Royal Victorian Eye and Ear Hospital, affectionately known in Melbourne simply as 'the Eye and Ear'.

At about the same time, Rod Saunders was being wakened by the nursing staff to begin the final preparations before undergoing major surgery. They needn't have bothered rousing him. He never really got to sleep that night. Perhaps it was the unfamiliarity of the hospital surrounds, but more likely, he thought, it was just nerves. Since an automobile accident in 1977 had left him profoundly deaf, he had never adapted to his loss of hearing. He was, on that day, perhaps the one person even more desperate than Professor Clark for the bionic ear to work.

When Graeme Clark first contacted Rod to consider the possibility of being a candidate for an experimental cybernetic ear implant, Rod had not hesitated. His mind was made up even before he fully understood what was involved. Rod was an ideal candidate for several reasons, two of which were related to his accident. Unlike many of the profoundly deaf, Rod's accident had left him with no hearing whatsoever. This meant that if Rod heard anything after the surgery, Clark and his team could be certain it was due to the implant and not to any residual hearing. Also, because Rod became deaf through an accident as an adult, it meant he knew what words sounded like and could compare any sounds he heard after the surgery with his experience of previous hearing sensations.

After months of tests and interviews with a select number of possible candidates, Rod was ecstatic when his wife received the call that he had been selected as the first bionic ear recipient. Rod viewed the long hours of surgery his body was about to endure as simply a necessary hurdle along the path to being able to hear again.

Graeme Clark was not a man to leave anything to chance. Others might have attempted the operation earlier, but Graeme was meticulous about every aspect of research and preparation. In fact, Graeme was meticulous about nearly everything. Whatever he undertook, even the selection of a house site and the building of a family home, was done on the basis of careful research and planning. The only notable exception was his penchant for purchasing second-hand vehicles with unique and sometimes endearing faults. But when it came to his science, nothing less than thorough preparation was acceptable.

Graeme had refused to hurry his preparation for this day, even when teams overseas, encouraged in part by his published research over the last decade, joined the race to produce a bionic ear. He had taken the time, of necessity, to become a multi-specialist in inner ear surgery, cybernetics, electronic engineering, speech processing and neuroscience. He had tested and retested the implant and its components. He had searched carefully for a surgical candidate who was ideally suited. He had devised a way to reduce the risk of infection during such a long and difficult surgery by setting up the operating theatre to have sterile air blown continuously over the patient.

Finally, he had practised the procedure repeatedly with his carefully chosen surgical team. Brian Pyman, a gifted ear surgeon, was one of the first colleagues to support Clark in his vision of developing a bionic ear. He and Brian had practised fifty temporal bone dissections in preparation for the procedure. George Domaigne, who would be the anaesthetist, was one of the best in his field.

As Clark entered the operating theatre he was greeted by his old mentor, Gerard Crock, professor of ophthalmology, who had supported Graeme from the beginning of Graeme's own appointment as professor of otolaryngology at the Eye and Ear. Crock said, 'The moment of truth has arrived, Professor Clark.' Somehow, he managed to make the statement sound reassuring.

When everything was prepared they sent for Rod Saunders. An orderly wheeled him into the surgical preparation room and Clark turned his attention immediately to the patient. As a rule, surgeons are not to get close to their patients. It makes it difficult to operate with the calmness and detachment necessary for complex surgical procedures. But Clark had spent many hours with Rod in interviews and doing tests and had developed a genuine affection for him. He knew how much this operation meant to Rod, and he also knew there were great risks. 'I assured him as best I could,' Graeme recalls. 'I was very conscious that he, too, was going into the unknown.' At that point both he and Rod were amazingly at peace, though, as Graeme now recalls with a wry smile; in Rod's case that may have had something to do with the fact he had just been administered 15 milligrams of Valium.

Once Rod was at ease, George Domaigne put the mask over his mouth and nose and began the process of anaesthetisation. Clark and his team waited patiently until the 'all clear' came from Domaigne, who would remain on hand throughout the surgery monitoring Rod's vital signs. Clark remembers very clearly what happened next.

I asked Sister Martin for the scalpel, took a deep breath, and pressed firmly downwards while sliding the knife along the path I had planned behind the ear. The skin gently parted, revealing the familiar anatomy of the underlying tissues. Then, carefully dissecting the lining of the ear canal from the bone, I lifted the ear-drum forward so that I could see into the middle ear. I was relieved to find a large, round window, the site for later inserting the stimulating electrodes into the inner ear . . . I turned my attention to drilling most of the air cells out of the mastoid bone so that I could expose the round window from behind, and make a bed for the implant package. For the next hour . . . the operating theatre was filled with the screeching of the drill and the whistling of the sucker as I removed bone dust and the irrigating water used to prevent the bone from overheating with high-speed drilling.[1]

Clark used the facial nerve, as planned, as a guide leading him into the middle ear. He was then able to turn his attention to making a bed for the receiver-stimulator, the 13-millimetre-thick package containing all the electronics necessary to receive radio signals from outside the body. This would need to be placed into the bone of the skull in such a way that it didn't bulge too much under the skin, but as Rod's skull was just 8 millimetres thick at this point it meant drilling to the very covering of the brain with utmost precision. Clark felt he was walking a tightrope. Regardless of all the hours of practice and all his previous surgeries, he knew the dangers of working so close to the brain. Finally he had created enough space for the package. But after four hours of surgery he was also beginning to feel weary, and exchanged places with Brian Pyman so that the surgery could continue with a fresh mind and steady hands.

Pyman began to insert the electrode bundle of wires into the inner ear. He began with a dummy electrode bundle that wound, as planned, some 25 millimetres into the inner ear—far enough, Clark had calculated, to stimulate all the important speech frequencies. Clark and Pyman exchanged a quick glance—they were nearly there. They used a micro-claw that Clark had developed specially for this procedure. (When the device later became commonplace for use in such operations, Graeme resisted efforts by colleagues to call it the 'Clark Claw'.) The electrode bundle was delicately inserted into the inner ear, and the package carefully placed in its bed. After both surgeons were satisfied there was no bleeding, they sutured the wound. They had been operating for almost nine hours.

It was over. Clark felt exhilaration and relief. Back at the University of Melbourne's Department of Ear, Nose and Throat Surgery, where Rod's family and staff members had been watching the entire historic operation via closed circuit television, there was also visible relief and excitement.

Rod began to waken slowly about an hour later. He was pleased to see Professor Clark standing by his bedside. He could tell by the look on the surgeon's face that the operation had gone as well as could be expected. Clark, for his part, was relieved to see Rod smile and speak with normal facial expressions. This meant that no nerves had been damaged during the delicate procedure. There was nothing to do now but wait. It would take four weeks for the ear to heal sufficiently in order to test the implant.

A week after the surgery Graeme was at the hospital in his office when he heard over the loudspeaker that there was a medical emergency on the fourth floor, where Rod was recovering. One of his colleagues had warned him before the surgery, 'You could kill your patient.' These words were ringing in his ears as he raced up the stairs. As he reached the fourth floor his worst fears were realised. It was Rod's room that was the centre of attention.

Graeme rushed in to find that Rod had collapsed on the floor, and the nursing staff now had him stretched out beside his bed, still semiconscious. Could this be it? Had all his precautions to prevent complications been in vain? Had he drilled too close to the brain? Could the strain of the long surgery have been too much? The young resident on duty was in a bit of a state about what to do, so Graeme stepped in and began to check Rod's vital signs to determine what had happened.

In the end, it turned out that while the nurse was changing Rod's dressing he had simply fainted. Greatly relieved, Graeme helped Rod back into his bed, none the worse for his fall.

The next three weeks passed more quietly. Rod returned home to recover, and Graeme spent time with his family, returning to his childhood home of Camden for some much needed relaxation with Margaret and their four daughters. He spent long hours walking through familiar countryside, praying and thinking about what was to come next. As Graeme recalled:

> Going back to the place of my youth with all its wonderful memories was always refreshing. I don't think I ever needed a holiday as much as that one. The years of tension in trying to get the prototype bionic ear developed had built up. At last I could feel that whatever the result it had finally been implanted. We now had the mammoth task of seeing if it was possible to get the patient to understand running speech.[2]

Despite Professor Crock's words of support to him before the surgery, Graeme knew that in a few short weeks the 'real' moment of truth would arrive. The surgery had been successful, but did the cochlear implant work? Could a small bundle of only ten electrodes actually stimulate the approximately 20,000 nerve endings responsible for hearing? And could Rod make sense of these signals in order to distinguish tone, vowels, consonants and, ultimately, words?

When Rod Saunders returned to hospital three weeks later with his wife Margaret for his first session of testing, he found an array of scientists, doctors, technicians and equipment. Up to a dozen people were crowded in and around the small room at the Otolaryngology[3] Department where the tests were to take place.

Rod sat in front of a computer screen while Joe Tong, a young mechanical engineer, sat in front of another screen beside him. The team's senior engineer, Jim Patrick, and his colleague Ian Forster were in an adjoining room, one whole wall of which was filled with a bank of computers that were programmed to process the sounds Rod was expected to hear via the gold box that had been implanted behind his ear. Professor Clark recalls that he gently fitted a headpiece onto Rod's head, positioning it so that its small transmitting aerial lay over the aerial of the implanted receiver-stimulator, which he had to do by feel through the swelling.

The best way to communicate with Rod was by writing. So Joe Tong, sitting at the computer beside Rod, wrote, 'Watch the screen. When the sign comes up, that means a signal has been sent through and we want to know if you've heard it. We'll be testing each electrode in turn.' The equipment was turned on and the signals sent. The signs flashed onto Rod's screen one by one, but he kept shaking his head. Despite turning the volume up and adjusting the signals, Rod heard nothing at all.

The team tested the ten different electrodes individually. Not a single sound. It was clearly not what Rod or anyone else expected. Rod could see the disappointment on everyone's faces, especially Professor Clark's. Joe Tong began writing on the pad, then held the paper up for Rod to read: 'Back to the drawing board.'

The tests were repeated a couple of days later, but still no positive result. The cochlear multi-electrode implant that Graeme had worked on to the exclusion of almost all else for the past twelve years had failed to stimulate a single sound sensation in Rod's brain!

Could it be, Clark wondered, that after all the planning, testing and development, the bionic ear did not work at all? But this was contrary to all his research and preliminary tests. The fact that something had been overlooked or not taken into consideration hardly seemed possible. Clark could not fathom why no positive result had been detected. After going through the myriad possibilities again and again in his mind, he was left with just one conclusion. Even though he knew the equipment had been thoroughly tested, he asked Jim Patrick and Ian Forster to recheck the equipment once more.

To the great relief of all, this time they found a fault. There was a single loose connection in the equipment. It explained why Rod had not been able to detect any sound at all. The problem was fixed and Rod was called back for another attempt. With great anticipation the equipment was again turned on and the signals sent. This time Rod indicated that he heard sounds. Each of the ten electrodes was tested and each found to produce a result. The team was relieved, as was Rod. It was enough for one session.

But could Rod actually distinguish sounds so as to recognise them? Rod returned on 18 September for the next series of tests. It was now six weeks since the surgery. Clark and the team decided to try something different. Without telling Rod what they were attempting, Clark's team used the computer to transmit the tune of Australia's then national anthem, 'God Save the Queen'. As soon as they began to send the transmission Rod surprised everyone by standing to attention, pulling out several of the leads attached to the external stimulating and monitoring equipment in the process! Rod, it turned out, was not only patriotic, but also had a sense of humour.

The bionic ear worked, at least with pitch and melody. For their next test Clark's team decided to switch the tune to Australia's unofficial 'second' national anthem, 'Waltzing Matilda', to prevent another patriotic display of wire removal. This time, if Rod recognised the tune, they wanted to ensure that they were able to record the event and gather data.

The question that now remained was whether Rod could make out words. This, after all, was the ultimate goal: to code speech with artificial electrical stimuli so it could be understood. Rod's brain had to learn to interpret the sounds it was hearing, and this would take some practice. The team worked with him through vowel and consonantal sounds. Finally, after several sessions, the ultimate test came. Rod was presented with groups of previously untested words and sentences. Clark recalls: 'I waited with bated breath as the material was presented.' If Rod couldn't make out words, then the device would have little practical application. The profoundly deaf would still be largely locked out of the world of the hearing.

Words and sentences were read out slowly, then the team waited for Rod to say what he heard. When Angela Marshall, who lectured in the university's new course in audiology, read out the word 'ship', Rod thought she said 'chat'. When she read 'goat', Rod thought she said 'boat', which was, Graeme thought to himself, nearly correct. Then she read the word 'raw' and Rod correctly identified it. When it became clear that Rod could recognise a number of words and sentences, Professor Clark excused himself and went into the adjoining room. He closed the door behind him and wept for joy. The bionic ear worked!

A milestone in medical science had been achieved. It was the first successful human cybernetic implant. There was, of course, still much to be done. A portable device was still to be developed that was practical for recipients to carry with them instead of sitting in a room with a bank of computers; surgeons would need to be trained in implanting the cochlear devices; and production of transistorised and affordable receiving units needed to be achieved. Clark knew that for their breakthrough to have an impact the implants would need to be affordable, and those with the implants could not rely on rooms full of computer banks to be available whenever they needed to communicate. Nevertheless, bionics had passed from the realm of science fiction to that of practical science. Hundreds of thousands of profoundly deaf people around the globe would, for the first time in human history, have the possibility of accessing the world of sound.

CHAPTER 2

Childhood in Camden

Camden today is an outer suburban extension of Sydney, lying just beyond Campbelltown in Sydney's south-west, nestled upon a rise inside a bend of the Nepean River. When Graeme Milbourne Clark was born on 16 August 1935 in the family home at 62 John Street, however, Camden was a country town of approximately three thousand residents. Being in Camden meant the family was close enough to Sydney to take advantage of its many cultural and intellectual offerings. But it was also far enough from Sydney to be a genuine country town. The Clark children recall riding their bicycles for miles into the countryside, at times as far as Campbelltown, some 8 miles distant. They often had weekend picnics along the Nepean River, and regular hiking trips in the nearby Blue Mountains.

Graeme's father Colin met his future wife, Dorothy May Thomas, at Stroud, New South Wales, soon after he had set up a local chemist shop. Colin established the business after topping his class in practical preparation at the Victorian College of Pharmacy in Melbourne. The fact that Colin remained in Stroud at all after his first visit to the town was something of an accident. He arrived late at night to look into buying a pharmacy because Russell Donald, a friend whose mother was a pharmacist, said there might be an opening in the town. It was the Depression and opportunities were rare so he had to pursue openings wherever they might be. When he saw the next morning just how small the town was, he determined he could not run a successful business there and decided to leave. But Stroud was so small that he was not able to get a train out that day and had to extend his stay, during which time the locals convinced him to remain. Colin decided to buy the local newsagency as well, and was able to combine the two small businesses into one large enough to be viable. It was an unusual combination, but if the news made the locals feel ill, he reasoned, at least they didn't have far to go to seek a remedy.

Dorothy had come to Stroud to spend a couple of weeks holidaying from her home in Sydney. She had been an art student at the Julian Ashton Art School, specialising in watercolours, before switching to the Sydney Conservatorium, where she studied piano. As it happened, the local banker in Stroud was having a 'musical evening' for young people and invited Colin, as one of the town's eligible young bachelors. He was hopeful Colin would become better acquainted with his daughter. They organised a gifted violinist for the evening but she needed an accompanist. When the family learned that a pianist from the Conservatorium was in town on holiday they took advantage of the opportunity to gain her services, not realising what havoc this decision would play with their matchmaking efforts.

Both Colin and another young bachelor were taken with the visiting young pianist and volunteered to walk her home that evening. Afterwards, Colin commented to his friend, 'Whoever marries that girl will be a very lucky man.' But Colin had already taken steps to ensure he would be that man: he had had the foresight to secure her address. After some correspondence, Dorothy was persuaded that

Stroud was a good location for another holiday. Romance soon blossomed and, after a courtship of nearly two years, Colin and Dorothy, both aged twenty-seven, were married. They remained briefly in Stroud before moving to Camden in 1934, where they would raise a family and spend the rest of their lives.

In Camden, Colin purchased the pharmacy on Argyle Street next to Whitemans' department store, which was a well-known landmark in the region. Dorothy began to offer music lessons and continued her watercolour painting. For Colin, pharmacy was something of a second choice in careers. He had initially wanted to study medicine but his family felt they could not afford it. So he directed his interests to pharmacy, and later studied optometry, which he practised from his Argyle Street shop.

Just around the corner and up the street from the chemist shop was the Clark family home. It was a simple, three bedroom double-brick house with a vegetable garden and swing set in the backyard, an external toilet and, courtesy of the Second World War and the proximity of the Camden Aerodrome, an air-raid shelter. Colin and Dorothy were able to build the house with the help of a loan from their neighbours, the Whitemans, whose boys, Ray and Ken, would play a big role in Graeme's childhood.

By today's standards the house was very basic, with the exception of the air-raid shelter. But for the three Clark children it was a fantastic home in which to grow up. Graeme, the firstborn, made use of every inch of space the house and yard provided. He admits to being somewhat 'hyperactive' and must have been a real handful for his parents. From the time he could speak he was always asking, 'What can I do now?' The boundless energy Graeme took into his career in medical science was always present. His sister Robin notes that she didn't start walking until she was two. 'I didn't need to,' she says with a smile. 'Graeme had enough energy for the both of us.'[4]

And if there wasn't enough to do or Graeme was unhappy with the direction things were taking he would take matters into his own hands. In a treasured family photograph Graeme is pictured, aged two, with a suitcase in each arm walking down the driveway. Things were not going as he wanted, so he was leaving home!

The house at 62 John Street was filled with happy childhood memories, and both Graeme and Robin particularly were somewhat saddened when the family's success allowed them to move to a larger home at the top of the street when Graeme was fifteen.

Graeme and Robin both remember Camden fondly as 'an incredible microcosm of society' and 'a wonderful place to grow up'. It was a close-knit community, into the fabric of which their parents were firmly embedded. Like any community, Camden had its share of characters. The generosity and hospitality of Colin and Dorothy Clark ensured that many of these became part of their children's world. One of the characters they recall was Toby Taplan, the council street sweeper. Toby took an interest in young Graeme because Graeme played the mouth organ—Toby referred to him as Larry Adler, who was a famous mouth organ player. But Toby was seen as belonging to the lower classes, and the class system was still very strong in towns like Camden in that era.[5] So many people simply didn't associate with him. But when Toby came by with his horse-drawn cart to collect the rubbish, Graeme and Robin remember that their mother always offered him something to drink and chatted with him. This was something that simply wasn't done by most at that time.

Another character known in town simply as 'the Tramp' stopped by regularly to get sponge cake from their mother, and also often stopped by their father's chemist shop for a meal. The Clark children also recall Florrie Gillespie, a spinster who helped their mum with the laundry, all done in those days in a copper tub. Florrie became a part of the household and when the Clarks moved house they helped her build a modest home on a small block of land in South Camden.

Behind Dorothy Clark's charitable and egalitarian ways was a rich and uniquely Australian pedigree. She was descended from John Small and Mary Parker, two prominent transportees from the First Fleet. In those days being descended from convicts, even First Fleeters, did not advance one's social status and was generally kept quiet. Her family did, however, take much pride in the fact that one of Dorothy's uncles, Eric Youdale, was decorated for bravery on the beaches of Gallipoli.

Another, Dorothy's uncle Alfred, received the Military Cross and two bars in the First World War. He, too, had fought at Gallipoli, but became ill and was returned home. When he recovered he joined the Royal Air Force (RAF) and was sent to Egypt where he spent a total of six weeks training as a pilot. He proved a natural aviator and flew a number of missions against the Germans. Receiving the Military Cross and two bars effectively means he received the Military Cross three times. He died during his last mission near the end of the war. The family is very proud of his war record and bravery, but have long been disappointed that his name does not appear on the honour roll in Canberra because of bureaucratic rules that did not count him as an Australian because he flew with the British RAF as there was no Royal Australian Air Force at that time.

But few in Camden would have been aware of these family connections. Dorothy was known in Camden not for her lineage but her charity, her skills as a pianist, and her watercolours.

Colin, like his wife, had a reputation for generosity at his chemist shop and let many a bill ride until his customers could pay. Colin's generosity and charity made an impression on his children. Graeme recalls that what struck him most about his father was his 'honesty and integrity, and the genuine, quiet interest he took in his customers'.

Quite often, Graeme recalls, 'tramps'—as they were called in those days—would come into the shop asking for money or food. 'They were always directed to the nearby café at Dad's expense.' He never sent anyone away without help.

Generosity and compassion for those in difficulty were apparently inherited traits. Colin's Scottish grandfather William Clark had been a shopkeeper in Newstead, Victoria, during the gold rush years. He was once held up by Ben Hall, a notorious bushranger. Hall had been a successful grazier running stock on a 40 square kilometre station south of Forbes in New South Wales. When his wife ran off with a stockman, taking their infant son with her, Hall's life deteriorated. He was forced to sell his property to a local politician to pay his debts and turned to a life of crime. He gained notoriety after being involved in the successful robbery of a transport of 2700 ounces of gold worth £14,000. He became known as brave Ben Hall and was celebrated for having never killed anyone in his raids, though the same could not be said for some of his accomplices.

When Hall held up the wagon of William Clark he asked whether he was William Clark the shopkeeper, who was well known for 'grub-staking' his poorer mining customers. That is to say, he let them run up a tab for food and supplies on the promise they would pay up with interest if they ever found gold. Of course, it was understood that most never would. His victim confirmed he was the same William Clark. The bushranger said he didn't want to rob such a decent man and rode off empty-handed. The story became a well-known family anecdote demonstrating the importance of generosity. Ben Hall continued his life of crime until police, with the help of Aboriginal trackers, finally caught up with him and killed him on 5 May 1865 at just twenty-seven years of age.

The charity of the Clark home extended also to a nineteen-year-old schoolteacher named Patricia Hider who found herself alone in

Camden in her first teaching job. They entertained her regularly in their home and introduced her around the town.

'They more or less adopted me,' she recalls. 'They made that time so much easier.'

This was probably never truer than when, later, Patricia suffered the loss of her newlywed husband, a pilot she had met while he was training at the local aerodrome. Sadly, he was killed in action only weeks after his deployment in the Pacific. It was, in fact, Colin Clark who was given the difficult task of informing Patricia of her husband's death.

Patricia never forgot the Clarks' hospitality, nor did she forget their son Graeme, who was among her first batch of Kindergarten and Year One students. Graeme, recalls Patricia, was a very bright boy and halfway through the year the school decided to move him up a grade level. For Patricia this meant losing a favourite student. 'He was a lovely student. He made the class very special. I was sorry to see him moved up,' she says. For young Graeme, being moved up meant he was always a year younger than his classmates—a situation to which he adapted remarkably well, with the possible exception of when he was on the rugby field. Decades later Graeme sits in the family room of his home looking at a rugby team photo from his first year at boarding school.

'That's me kneeling in the front row,' he points out. 'The little guy. I didn't relish getting tackled by that lot. It was the one time I found it a disadvantage being younger than my classmates.'

The rugby experience was one of the few challenges that daunted Graeme as a child. He was bright, athletic and adventurous. He joined the local branch of the cub scouts as soon as he was eligible and, like everything else, he gave it his full commitment, managing to win every possible merit badge save one. He missed his swimming badge because his legs were too heavy to float on the surface for the required ten seconds, and the swimming supervisor, his old Year One teacher

Patricia Hider, wouldn't bend the rules for anyone, not even Graeme. He excelled both in team sports and on the athletic field. So keen was young Graeme that he set up a high jump in his backyard to practise. This intense commitment to everything he turned his hand to would remain an abiding feature of Graeme's life and work.

With regard to his high jump training, however, his commitment to practice and perfection did not have good results. He landed badly in one of his jumps, injuring his neck. The lifelong recurrent pain he would experience as a result of this accident meant that it would make it very difficult for him to bend over a patient for long periods of time to perform surgery. Fortuitously for the history of medicine, the pain from this childhood injury was one of the decisive factors that, years later, would force Graeme to move from a promising career in the practice of surgery to one of medical research.

Graeme's adventurous spirit caused him, on occasion, other troubles as well. His friendship with the Whiteman boys next door often led him to push the boundaries: from building tunnels and forts with bags of chaff—which they were very lucky did not collapse on them— at the Whitemans' store, to surreptitious swims in the Nepean, to sneaking off to try their hand at smoking. The last misadventure finally brought them undone. After gathering enough tobacco from discarded cigarettes, they went to a café where they bought rolling paper, ostensibly for their parents. All that was then needed was a discreet place to smoke their cigarettes. They chose a spot along the Nepean, among the tall corn in local farmer Fred Skinner's vegetable patch. Unfortunately, the rising smoke was seen by Mr Skinner, who thought his field was on fire, and came in haste to put it out. He was not pleased with what he discovered, and duly notified the parents of those involved. While Graeme did not relish the trouble he was in with his parents, getting caught did have the benefit of bringing a quick end to his cigarette smoking.

For Graeme, growing up in Camden as the eldest son of Colin and Dorothy Clark was a happy childhood which he remembered fondly in later years. But his childhood in Camden also played a vital role in shaping his character and providing him with the ambition to study medicine. When not out hiking, swimming, playing sport or getting into mischief with the Whiteman boys, Graeme enjoyed spending time listening to his mother's collection of classical music and reading some of the many books his parents had collected.

The biographies of Marie Curie and Louis Pasteur made a big impression on him, reinforcing his early desire to study medicine. Pasteur particularly fascinated Graeme 'with his beautiful yet simple experiments that showed why wine fermented. He didn't stop at fermentation, but demonstrated how vaccination could prevent anthrax and cholera in animals. He spent many hours finding out how to immunise against rabies . . . He had to risk vaccinating a young boy before the vaccine was completely proven, and saved his life.' Most of us would simply stand in awe at Pasteur's accomplishments. But Clark, even as a young boy, had a very different response. Graeme thought, 'If he could do those things, I wondered, why couldn't I?'[6] Indeed, it was from Pasteur that Graeme learned that there were only two kinds of research: good research and bad research. It was a lesson he would carry with him into his long career as a research scientist.

Thus inspired by Curie and Pasteur, Graeme decided to set up his own laboratory in his mother's laundry. At age nine, young Graeme was already experimenting by translating fluids from diseased tomato plants to healthy ones using a syringe he made himself with blowing glass and a cork plunger. As always, Graeme was very hands-on with regard to knowledge. It wasn't enough to learn about something from books. He had to try it out himself to see how and why it worked.

Graeme's experiments continued and their complexity increased. The family laundry grew to look more like a science laboratory than a place for washing clothes. The arrangement of using the laundry as his laboratory continued into Graeme's medical school days—though his mother must have been horrified by some of the things that ended up being stored on her shelves. Years later, when his father was cleaning out the laundry and Graeme's old makeshift laboratory, he discovered various bones and human body parts preserved in jars—including a brain. He wasn't sure whether to call the hospital, the police or the morgue!

Graeme's early interest in medicine was such that, during his later primary school years, when he and the other children played army— as was popular among boys during the Second World War—Graeme always volunteered to play the medic. 'If the enemy scored a direct hit or there were shrapnel injuries, it was assumed that I would know what to do,' he recalls. It was an unusual boy, especially during the war years, who would rather take up the medical kit than the wooden sticks used for guns when playing with his mates in the schoolyard.

When the minister of the local Methodist church, where the Clark family were members, asked Graeme what he wanted to be when he grew up, he expected Graeme to say he wanted to be a C class steam engine driver, as many boys his age wanted to do. Graeme surprised the minister by saying he wanted to be an ear and eye doctor—a very specific goal for a ten-year-old. But just how did a young boy from Camden become so determined to become an ear doctor? To answer that question we need to take a closer look into the Clark family.

CHAPTER 3

'When I grow up, I'm going to fix ears'

If Graeme's minister was surprised by his early passion for medicine, particularly his desire to be an ear doctor, Patricia Hider, his Year One teacher at primary school, was not. She recalls asking each of her thirty or so students at Camden Central School what they wanted to do when they grew up. She was particularly struck by the earnestness of young Graeme's response. 'When I grow up,' he confidently told his teacher, 'I'm going to fix ears.'

'And do you know what?' Patricia says, her ninety-year-old voice bursting with pride as she tells the story, 'He did!'

In order to understand how Graeme came to such a clear and specific vision at such a young age, we must turn our attention again to Graeme's father, Colin Clark.

More than any other person, Colin Clark was responsible for his son's desire to study medicine and specialise in the problem of deafness. Colin's own early interest in medicine certainly was an influence. It was the reason the household had biographies of Marie Curie and Louis Pasteur on hand. Colin's work with pharmaceuticals made practical medicine familiar in the Clark household. Colin even produced his own brand of medicine, 'Colmark', under which he sold cough syrups and other remedies. It is no accident that Colin's eldest son went on to become an ear, nose and throat surgeon, and his daughter Robin and youngest son Bruce went on to become pharmacists; with Robin first serving as a retail pharmacist before transferring to ward pharmacy, and Bruce eventually taking over the family pharmacy in Camden.

Dorothy gave her children an appreciation for art and music. In Graeme's words: 'She showed me the value of creativity.' But the interest in medicine and science that shaped the professional lives of all three Clark children came from Colin.

From a very young age Graeme helped his father out at the chemist shop. At first this was just a matter of a young boy wanting to be with his father, but as Graeme's interest in his father's work grew, so did his responsibilities, until this became his regular after-school and holiday job. Graeme, in fact, was so often at the chemist shop, and usually involved in some sort of experiment at the back, that the assistants working at his father's shop nicknamed him 'the Bunsen burner boy'.

Graeme's work with his father made medicinal and chemical terms familiar to him. Graeme learned much about various ailments and remedies. He can still cite these early practical lessons: 'Magnesium and calcium carbonate relieved indigestion, and potassium citrate made the urine alkaline for kidney and bladder infections. Senega and ammonia loosened the secretions with a cough, and rhubarb root or senna pods made the bowels run if you were constipated. For a tonic or general pick-me-up, one of the best ingredients was liquor of strychnine. Sometimes,' Graeme recalls, 'the doctor would even add a little brandy [to the script] without the patient knowing.'[7] As a youth (with a good Methodist upbringing) he found it amusing when strict teetotallers would come back asking for more medicine, remarking how great it was!

His father's work as an optometrist presented Graeme with one of his first real opportunities for learning about the human body. Graeme recalls that his father would allow him to look through the equipment and view the human eye. He was thrilled to be able to see the retina and wanted to understand how it worked. Graeme credits these experiences with awakening his early interest in becoming a doctor. But Colin influenced his son even more profoundly in another way.

Colin Clark, the popular and successful local chemist, was severely deaf. At a time before effective and affordable hearing aids were available, this presented serious problems for his work and social life. Colin began having hearing problems as a young man, first noticing difficulty when he was just twenty-two. He went to his family doctor in Glen Innes, thinking he had a problem with wax build-up. 'You don't have any wax,' the doctor said, 'but if you try holding your nose and blowing up your cheeks to pop your ears, that might help.' It didn't. Five years later, in 1932, the situation had worsened, so Colin went to see a specialist in Macquarie Street, Sydney.

The doctor confirmed his worst fears. He was suffering irreversible hearing loss and the problem was degenerative. Colin knew enough about the condition to realise how serious the matter was, and how difficult it would make his life. He had only recently proposed to Dorothy, and he determined to be bluntly honest with her about his condition. He felt she would be foolish to go through with the marriage and wanted to give her a way out.

'You know I'm deaf and the doctors say it's only going to get worse. If you don't want to marry me,' he told her, 'I'll understand.' But Dorothy would not be put off, and the two soon married as planned.

Colin had to listen very carefully to everything, and had great difficulty in crowds and at social gatherings. Many times people would greet him on the street and he would not respond—giving the unfortunate impression that he was being rude. Work at the chemist shop was also difficult. Listening carefully all day long required very great effort and by the end of the day Colin would be exhausted. Dorothy used to comment, 'It's such a nervous strain.' Yet Colin didn't complain. He made the best of his circumstances. And his disability certainly didn't keep him away from a lifelong commitment to the Camden community. Among other things, Colin found time to be a foundation member of the Rotary Club, the founding chairman of the Camden Historical Society, and a member of the board of the Carrington Hospital.

To his family, Colin seldom seemed embarrassed by his deafness. But his oldest son found it difficult at times. Graeme recalls that many customers at his father's shop wanted to be discreet about what they needed. He especially remembers those customers who wanted to buy a contraceptive. His father would often ask them to repeat their request more loudly, causing great embarrassment. On the days when Graeme would help his father in the shop he would often indicate to his father that he had heard the request and went to get the medicine or item in order to avoid embarrassment to the customers. Perhaps for this reason Colin found his work with optometry much more to his liking, as he was less reliant on his hearing to do the job well.

At home, Colin's deafness also had an impact on family life. Even in the early years of marriage, Colin would sleep through the babies' cries, leaving his wife with the task of getting up during the night with the children. Much conversation and interaction with the family was also missed. In one memorable family anecdote, Graeme relates how the family was on holiday in Oberon, west of the Blue Mountains in the New South Wales Central Tablelands. They spent the night in a hotel during the height of the pea-picking and shearing seasons. That night there was a lot of yelling and fighting by local shearers and pea-pickers outside the door of the hotel room. Dorothy became so concerned the door would be broken down and the family attacked that she stacked all available furniture up against the door. The next morning Colin awoke, perplexed at the pile of furniture barricading the door to their hotel room. He hadn't heard a thing and had slept soundly through the night. While the story was the source of much amusement in the family, Colin's deafness was often the cause of embarrassment and difficulty. Graeme remembers childhood friends visiting their home thinking his father was aloof, and the many occasions in which his father was simply not able to join in on a discussion or be a part of the conversation around him.

At this time effective hearing aids were not generally available in Australia, so there was little to be done for the condition. From as far back as the seventeenth century, hearing aids—in the form of large horns held up to the ear—were used to assist with hearing. These devices gained the height of their popularity in the mid-nineteenth century and still feature in comic-strip portrayals of those with hearing loss. Most, however, found them cumbersome and embarrassing. Certainly a pharmacist could not walk about his shop with one hand holding onto a large horn, and expect his customers to speak into it. Such a device would have been equally impractical around the family dinner table or any other setting with free-flowing conversation involving more than two people. By the end of the nineteenth century, those with hearing loss were pressing for smaller, more effective hearing aids. Recent advances in technology gave them hope that this was possible.

The invention of the telephone by Alexander Graham Bell in 1876, with its ability to electronically amplify sound using a carbon microphone and battery, lent much hope to the idea that progress could be made in this area. In fact, J.C. Chester, a hearing loss sufferer from Montana, is credited with producing the first portable electric hearing aid when he attached a battery to a modified Bell telephone, turned the volume up to maximum, and carried the device around with him. This, however, was hardly practical. Further progress was made when Thomas Edison invented the carbon transmitter in 1886. The key components for workable electric hearing aids were at last available.

The first commercial electric hearing aids appeared in 1898. The Dictograph Company was first on the market, making use of both Bell's and Edison's inventions. Later that year a device called the Akouphone was patented by Miller Reese Hutchison, and came onto the market in 1899. The Akouphone, which sold for the princely sum of US$400, was followed by a hearing aid device produced by the German company Siemens in 1913 and advertised as being about the size of a large cigar box. These devices were essentially electric speakers, similar to those used in telephones, and came with attachments that would fit into the ear.

The first vacuum tube hearing aid was patented in 1920 by Earl Hanson, a US naval engineer. The device was called a Vactuphone and used the earlier telephone technology to convert sound to electric signals, and then used a vacuum tube to amplify them. It weighed about 3 kilograms and was considered light enough to wear. Most came in leather cases with hand straps so that the user could carry it with them like a large purse. Further development along these lines continued in the 1920s and '30s, with the technological advances of the Second World War making it possible to create workable and easily wearable hearing aids that became commercially available soon after the war.[8]

It was one of these devices, sold by Angus & Coote in Sydney, that Colin Clark acquired in 1945, just after the end of the war. Despite all the progress, by today's standards it would be considered awkwardly large and of limited effectiveness. Yet it did help, and Colin was keen to keep up with technology as further advances were made. He did not have to wait long. In 1948 a team of Bell Laboratories engineers consisting of John Bardeen, Walter Brattain and William Shockley developed the transistor. This was a huge breakthrough for hearing aid technology as it meant large and less efficient vacuum tubes were no longer needed.

In 1952 the first transistorised hearing aids, which were actually hybrids containing both transistors and vacuum tubes, came onto the market. It was the advent of the modern hearing aid. Colin was able to acquire his first transistorised hearing aid in the early 1960s, when they became commercially viable in Australia. For Colin Clark and hundreds of thousands like him, they were life-changing devices. But at best they could only amplify sound to take advantage of residual hearing ability. For those with severe hearing loss, they could do only so much. For the profoundly deaf, they were of no assistance at all. That breakthrough was still another two decades off. The progression of hearing aids in the Clark home, however, and the technological advances in hearing aid technology that they represented, made an impression on Graeme.

Colin's interest in medicine and pharmaceuticals certainly influenced his eldest son in the choice of studying medicine. But it was without doubt Colin's own hearing loss that was decisive for the direction his son's medical career would take.

CHAPTER 4

Boarding school
in Sydney

Graeme didn't mind being a year ahead in school. He was the kind
of boy who relished a challenge and was only too eager to learn new
things. It did, however, have one distinct disadvantage. One of the
first dilemmas the Clarks faced when Graeme showed an interest in a
medical career was how to provide their son with the opportunity to
one day study medicine while living in a country town with no senior
high school. It meant the Clarks were faced with an awkward decision
when Graeme completed his primary schooling. The intermediate
school that existed at that time in Camden only covered three years
and was not designed to prepare students for university studies. But
could they send an eleven-year-old to and from Sydney every week?
They knew their son had much potential and a keen interest in
pursuing medicine, and they wanted to give him every opportunity
to pursue this path—an opportunity circumstances had denied his
father.

The Clarks did some searching about, much as parents would
do today, to find the most appropriate school for their son. As it

happened, the principal of Sydney Boys High School had a son who was a chemist and was known to Colin. The Clarks pursued this connection and Sydney Boys High School agreed to take Graeme on as a student, provided his parents could find relatives for him to stay with during the week in the city. Arrangements were made for Graeme to stay with his maternal grandparents, the Thomases, who lived in the Sydney suburb of Coogee.

Graeme's grandmother was very bright, and would have liked to have gone to university herself, but there were few opportunities for girls to do so in her time. Her academic abilities, however, meant she was able to help Graeme with his schoolwork, especially his French lessons. Graeme's grandmother also allowed him to go to the shops to buy comics. It was during this period that he discovered *Buck Rogers* and *Flash Gordon*. These stories opened up whole new worlds for Graeme. They helped him imagine a technological future where anything might be possible.

For Graeme, boarding with his grandparents during the week meant getting up every Monday morning at 6.30 in Camden. After a quick bite of breakfast and a splash of the face he would rush to the train station to catch the seven o'clock train to Sydney, an old steam train known affectionately as 'Puffing Billy'. It was a small train, and when there was ice on the tracks, which occurred regularly in winter, the passengers would have to get out and walk or sometimes even help push the train up the hill to Campbelltown. The 8-mile trip to Campbelltown on Puffing Billy took half an hour—providing there was no ice. Graeme would then switch trains to the Goulburn Express into Sydney, arriving at the Central Railway Station at 8.30 a.m. From there he met up with other boys who had converged on the station, and caught a tram up Chalmers Street through Strawberry Hills in time to arrive for the start of classes at nine o'clock. After school he would take the tram to Coogee to stay with his grandparents until

Friday afternoon, when he would make the long return journey to Camden.

It was, therefore, only on the weekends, amid all the homework he had to complete, that he was able to spend any time with his family, including his new baby brother, Bruce. It was a lot to ask of an eleven-year-old. But these were different times and such arrangements were not uncommon.

It was 1947 when Graeme began high school in Sydney. The war had only recently ended. The soldiers, many only having just been demobbed, had returned home and were settling back into their lives. The country, however, was still enduring many of the hardships and some of the shortages of wartime. The economy was making the transition back to peacetime and the massive postwar migration that changed the face of Australia was yet to begin in earnest. Australia was still very British, and sending off academically promising boys to all-male boarding schools at a young age was seen as something of a rite of passage.

Nevertheless, the experience of studying and living away from home was not always an easy one. Graeme recalls many a tear shed for home. This was particularly true when, due to his grandmother's worsening health, other arrangements needed to be made the following year. By that time Graeme had earned a scholarship that allowed him to become a boarder at The Scots College, in Sydney's eastern suburbs, with his only visits home now restricted to the term holidays. It meant, among other things, little time to hang out with his old friends, especially the Whiteman boys; little time to spend with his sister Robin; and little opportunity to get to know his baby brother Bruce, who was not two years old.

The switch to Scots College from Sydney Boys High School was a big change in many ways. The Scots College was established in 1893 by the Reverend Arthur Aspinall to meet the needs of the many

Graeme (aged 4 months) with his parents, Colin and Dorothy Clark, at Wilton, near Camden, New South Wales. His parents had to take Graeme for regular walks to keep him occupied.

Colin Clark in 1945 in the pharmacy he purchased in 1935 in Camden. Colin later expanded the business to include an optometrist centre for testing sight. Graeme enjoyed many hours after school helping his father and gained early exposure to the world of medicine.

At the age of eighteen months, Graeme announced he was bored, picked up his bags and said he was leaving home.

Graeme (aged 8) and his sister Robin (aged 5) in the backyard of their Camden home. Graeme and his sister spent much time together as children and have remained close.

Cub scouts was very popular in Australia in the 1940s. Graeme was a 'sixer' and leader of the red pack of cubs in Camden.

Graeme (centre, front) and the undefeated Royle House rugby team at Scots College, Sydney. He was the smallest and youngest member of the top house team.

The Scots College boat race, Penrith, 1951. Graeme was a keen participant in team sports and on the athletic field.

Margaret's 21st birthday celebration. Graeme proposed that evening.

Graeme and Margaret in 1960 outside his mother's laundry at 3 Menangle Road, Camden. Graeme used the laundry as a laboratory.

As a young married couple, finances were tight for the Clarks. They left Sydney on the maiden voyage of the *Oriana*, combining their honeymoon with a move to the United Kingdom, where Graeme took up postgraduate surgical studies.

Margaret and Graeme at the christening of their first daughter, Sonya Dorothy, on 29 March 1964.

Margaret and Graeme with their daughters Sonya, Cecily and Roslyn while in Sydney, 1969. They moved to Sydney so Graeme could complete his PhD research.

Graeme undertaking research in 1969 at the University of Sydney on the structural support of the nose to provide a basic understanding of how to do improved plastic surgery without loss of support of the nose.

Margaret and Graeme in Sydney in late 1969 celebrating his appointment to the chair of Otolaryngology in Melbourne. It was the first time they could afford to dine out during Graeme's time as a PhD student.

Graeme's PhD graduation from the University of Sydney in 1970. From left to right: Fred Burtenshaw, Margaret's stepmother Olive, Graeme and Margaret with Sonya, Cecily and Roslyn, Graeme's brother Bruce, and Dorothy and Colin Clark.

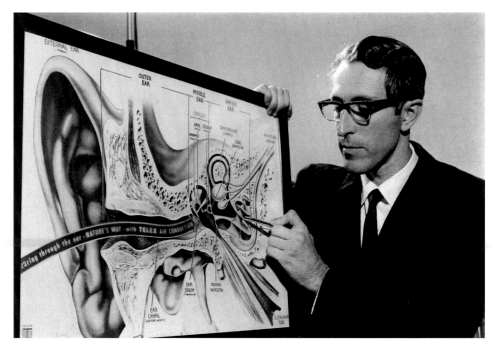

Graeme explains how he plans to restore hearing by stimulating the cochlea electrically. The concept was considered radical at the time. (*The Age*)

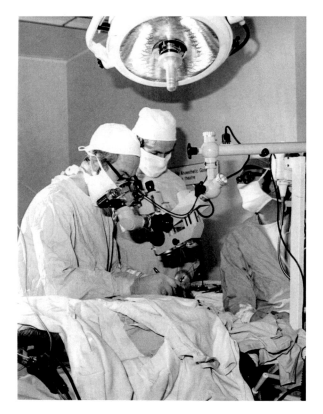

Graeme leading surgical study in 1972 in preparation for later human implants, assisted by Field Rickards and Don McMahon.

Scottish Presbyterian families who had settled throughout New South Wales. By the time Graeme Clark arrived there in the postwar years it was already one of Sydney's elite boys' boarding schools, and took in boys from a range of religious backgrounds—though attendance at the main Sydney Presbyterian church was still mandatory for all boarders. The Scottish Presbyterian heritage and ethos remained very strong.

Twelve-year-old Graeme often felt like he had been sentenced to confinement. During his first term the only bed that could be found was in a corridor of Aspinall House. The next term a regular bed was found for him in Royle House, one of the newest houses at Scots, having been founded only ten years earlier in 1938. The downside was that this house had the reputation of containing the toughest boys in the school. Graeme soon worked out that the way to be accepted and survive was through involvement in sports. Fortunately, even though he was a year younger than most of the other boys in his year level, he excelled at sport, particularly athletics and cricket. This eased his transition considerably.

Graeme even discovered that he was not too bad at rugby, despite his age and size. Rugby in Sydney at that time was a sport no boy could avoid. Everyone was expected to play, and when not playing they were expected to attend games and cheer for their school or house team. The competition between houses within Scots College was intense and Graeme's performance in the under thirteen A-grade team soon saw him promoted to the first house team in order to free up some of the better and larger players for other house teams in an attempt to win in each division. For a boy who felt out of his depth in the under thirteen A-grade side, competing against players several years his senior in the top house team was nothing short of overwhelming. The smallest member of the side, he was placed on the wing where it was hoped his speed and agility might bear results. For Graeme it wasn't so much a chance to be a hero as an opportunity to let the side down and become the laughing-stock of the house. What should have been every schoolboy's dream was shaping into a nightmare.

The moment of truth came when he was asked to put on the maroon of Royle House for its match against his old house, Aspinall. Early in the second half, one of Aspinall's largest players broke free with the ball and charged straight for the young, slightly built winger. Graeme knew what was at stake. He couldn't stop the giant but he at least had to make it look like he gave it a good effort if he was not to be blamed for letting the other team score a try. His intention was to go through the motions of a tackle, and the safest bet seemed to be to make a grab for the player's thighs as he sped past. This, he thought, should at least look like a genuine effort from the stands. Graeme ran to meet the charging opponent, closed his eyes, and grabbed blindly at thigh level. What he didn't see, with his eyes closed, was that just as he was about to go through the motions of a hopeless tackle, the opposing player leapt into the air to dive over Graeme towards the tryline. Instead of brushing past his waist, Graeme caught the player in midair by the ankles. The giant came thudding to the ground and the crowd of boys erupted.

Graeme had not only survived but had managed an unexpected and spectacular tackle. More importantly, he was now accepted in the school's toughest house, despite his young age and slight build. Of course, he dared never admit the whole thing was a fluke, accomplished with his eyes closed. The event is symbolic of much that was to come in Graeme's life. It was not the last time that a combination of skill, determination and sheer good luck would play a critical role in the turn of events.

Through strict routine, academic rigour, emphasis on sport, mandatory church services, and the camaraderie of the schoolhouse, boarding school was designed to turn boys into men. Like most boys (and girls) of that era who experienced the boarding house culture, Graeme's was not always a pleasant experience. There was little time for one's self, there were endless commitments and expectations, and long stints away from home.

One of the regular disciplines of the boarders was attendance every Sunday morning at St Stephen's Presbyterian Church on Macquarie Street in the city. The boys would rise early, take the bus in to the city centre, and sit in their assigned section. The minister, the Reverend Alan Tory, did not inspire enthusiasm in the boys—which in any event would have been difficult with a group of high school students who were told they must attend church. They dubbed him 'Bory Tory' and spent their time writing and drawing rather inappropriate things in their hymnals. Graeme recalls that the books would be collected and locked away each week after the service so as not to cause offence to any of the regular parishioners. It was an approach to church and Christianity that made it seem like just one more duty to which the boys had to attend. It did little to awaken anyone's faith, including Graeme's.

After the church service, Graeme had the only real opportunity for free time. Being good Scottish Presbyterians, there were no Sunday sporting commitments, and the boys were on their own for lunch and the afternoon. Graeme would catch the tram to Coogee, the same suburb where he had stayed during the week with his grandparents during his first year of high school. He went to his Uncle Keith and Aunt Kathleen Thomas's home and had lunch with them and their three daughters. Keith was his mother's brother, and it was refreshing after a week of boarding school to spend even a few hours feeling like part of a real family. Perhaps one of the most important outcomes of these Sunday afternoon visits were the many conversations with his Uncle Keith about his future. Graeme remembers how his uncle encouraged him to pursue his dream of studying medicine and becoming a doctor.

And if the routine for boarders at Scots College wasn't already demanding enough, in his final two years the school decided to make it mandatory to join the Army Cadets. 'As with football,' Graeme recalls, 'there was no escape.' Unlike his primary school days of playing army, there was no medic option. He had to practise real soldiering. He didn't relish the thought of killing anyone. He reminded himself that it was just simulation. Nevertheless, like everything else, he threw himself into it determined to do his best. The reward was the opportunity during the summer break before his final year at Scots to go to Singleton to attend Officer Training School. This meant that in his final year he got to boss the other cadets around and make them run laps with their rifles held over their heads. Like much else in those days, however, it was mostly just more expectations and commitments, and ever less free time. Needless to say, there was no time whatsoever for girls, and Graeme's teenage dating life, like that of most of his fellow students, was non-existent. As Graeme recalls:

On Saturday morning, it was off to play your game of football or cricket, and that might mean going half-way across Sydney by public transport. It was also compulsory to go and watch the school first football team play in the afternoon and barrack for them. Cheering for the school as it struggled for a place at the rowing regatta was mandatory. Then, on Saturday evening, we watched an out-of-date film in the school hall . . . This meant that we had little chance to develop our social skills with girls.[9]

While there were admittedly hardships, Graeme appreciated the opportunity his parents gave him to attend Scots. He was especially appreciative of the opportunity to learn under some very high quality teachers. Dr Simmons in chemistry and Fred Pollock in maths both made big impressions, as did Barney Cubis, the history teacher, who

34

often took Sunday evening chapel and exhibited a very genuine faith. But perhaps the biggest impact was made by his English teacher, Rhys Jones, whose 'fanatical' methods regarding summaries and inductive and deductive reasoning were critical in helping Graeme go on to achieve the success he did in medical school. Apart from the high quality of general academic preparation at Scots, the experience also taught him how to be disciplined in the organisation of his study time—a skill that would become very important in medical school. He also learned to develop a kind of toughness that he would need to draw upon heavily during the gruelling shifts of his hospital residency.

Despite the rigour of academic life, it was sport that left one of the most significant impressions on Graeme. While rugby was a real physical challenge that often wore his body down to the point of sickness, he found genuine enjoyment in his cricket, for which he was more naturally suited. He had practised his batting for years and as an adolescent back in Camden had studied Don Bradman's 1938 book on batting. One of his best memories from those high school years was playing in the school A-team as opening batsman. In those days, Graeme recalls, the batsmen didn't wear helmets. This meant there was always a very real risk of serious injury and he had to be constantly alert. Even in his final year of school, when studies left him no time to attend practice, his skill with the bat was such that his coach kept him in the A-team as opening batsman to face the fast bowlers.

Despite the absence of any sort of dating life, the mandatory church services and the strict study routine, Graeme has always looked back fondly on his days at Scots College, and still relishes the opportunity to return as an old scholar to speak to the students. For Graeme, an experience which began seeming like a sentence of confinement finished on a high note of academic and athletic success, and social enjoyment.

CHAPTER 5

Brains, bones and exams

In 1952 at the age of sixteen, Graeme Clark began his first year of undergraduate studies in medicine at the University of Sydney. His dream of becoming a doctor and helping people with hearing problems had taken a significant step forward. But before that dream could be realised there was much study to be done in a range of subjects—some of which Graeme struggled to see the significance of for training to become a doctor. How, Graeme found himself wondering in his first year of medical school, 'could the intestines of the hydatid worm, the sexual reproduction of a flowering plant, the chemical structure of alcohol, or the bending of light through a prism be relevant to the real issues of being a doctor?'[10]

Despite his concerns about some aspects of the curriculum, Graeme applied himself to his studies and performed well enough on his first-year exams to be invited to spend the summer as a prosector in anatomy. This was a real honour, as only the students who did well in their first-year exams were invited to do human dissections during the summer holidays. While it meant being unable to return home to

Camden for the holidays, he realised it was the kind of opportunity he could not pass up. At the end of the summer, his work was put on display at the University Anatomy Museum. Being chosen as a prosector provided an opportunity to become even more knowledgeable about human anatomy and the art of dissection.

During the summer program, Graeme was assigned two tasks: the dissection of the elbow, and the dissection of the hamstring muscles. The former would be used to demonstrate to student doctors and nurses what structures they needed to avoid when giving injections, the latter would be used to demonstrate the kinds of injuries common among football players.

One of the interesting experiences of his time as an anatomy student was the group to which he was assigned to work that summer. Already Australia was becoming a destination for Asian students—and group assignments for dissecting the human body were made on an alphabetical basis. This meant that Clark was assigned to work with Chang, Cheung and Chong. By the end of summer, Graeme recalls, he knew where to find every Chinese restaurant in Sydney. It was his first real introduction to the multicultural society that Australia was to become.

Graeme's interest in practical anatomy continued into his third year when the focus was on the study of the brain. To assist in his studies, Graeme bought a brain from the hospital mortuary (a practice since made illegal by the *Human Tissue Act*) and added it to the growing collection in his childhood laboratory—his mother's laundry back in Camden.

Anyone familiar with the study of medicine will know that the initial course of academic study in the classroom, while demanding, is merely preparation for the real test every would-be GP, specialist and surgeon is thrown into—residency. It was only in fourth year that the students spent any time in hospital wards. During summer holidays, Graeme was able to gain added practical experience in clinical medicine through the support and encouragement of one of the local Camden GPs, Dr Robert Crookston. Graeme recalls that Dr Crookston was the old-fashioned kind of GP who did everything. So not only was Graeme able to take blood and run tests for him in his small pathology laboratory, but he would also accompany him when he did his rounds in hospital. And on occasion he was even allowed to go into the operating theatre and assist with actual surgery. All this was not only great encouragement but helped Graeme better understand the kind of work for which he was preparing.

But before Graeme and the other students could begin to apply what they had been preparing so hard for, they had to get through their fourth-year exams. As a consistently good student, Graeme was not especially worried, and perhaps put a little less effort into preparations than he could have. This proved to be a mistake. The exams were much tougher than he had expected. As he was sitting them, he had a sinking feeling that his results may not be quite up to the mark. He was right. When the results of those who had passed all their exams were posted, Graeme's name was not among them. He had failed one of his core subjects.

The poor result in his fourth-year exams was a shock, and meant that he had to spend his summer holidays retaking a subject. Graeme was not used to failure. Perhaps success came too easily for him sometimes. But as a natural perfectionist, it was never good enough just to get through. To fail at something was an experience he hoped not to repeat. He determined to study more diligently and become a better student. In the end he not only passed the class, but vowed never to allow himself to get into that situation again. Graeme kept up his renewed focus and discipline to such an extent that two years later he topped the class in his final year of medicine. For Graeme, the experience of having to retake a subject was both frustrating and embarrassing. But it turned out to be one of those fortuitous failures that helped to shape the course of his future career.

In 1958 Graeme Clark finally began his first year of residency at the Royal Prince Alfred Hospital (RPA) in Sydney. Like the other young medical graduates, he had been told it would be difficult. But nothing could have prepared him for the volume of work required. It was the hardest he had ever worked in his life. His experiences are still typical of what many medical residents go through.

> There was no forty-hour week. While doing surgery I would often start at 8 a.m. on Monday, help with emergencies during the day and right through Monday night, assist at routine surgery all Tuesday, and then look after these patients until midnight—forty hours straight. I was on call for patients every second night and every second weekend. I also had to sleep at the hospital during the week, even when off-duty. I had to learn not to make mistakes although I was nearly falling asleep on my feet . . . Then, at night, there would be piles of patient histories waiting to be summarised.[11]

Despite all his hard work in that first year of residency, Graeme was quite surprised and disappointed not to be included on the list of those invited to do their senior year of residency at the Royal Prince Alfred. After topping his final year of medicine and gaining a first-year residency appointment at the RPA, Graeme had been looking towards a career as a physician, the 'thinking doctors', rather than that of a surgeon, the 'craftsmen'. Having to start over again as a senior resident at a new hospital meant that all the positions for physicians would have been filled by those continuing on at that hospital for their final year of residency. Graeme would have to settle for a residency in surgery. While he was never certain what led to his failure to be asked to stay on at the RPA, other than his youth and relative immaturity compared to the older residents, it proved again to be a fortuitous, career-changing failure. It was in surgery that Graeme was destined to make history—but without this crushing disappointment, he would likely have never gone down that path.

When his second-year residency appointment finally came through, he found himself assigned as a senior surgical resident at the Royal North Shore Hospital in Sydney, which at that time enjoyed the nickname among medical professionals of 'the country club'. The atmosphere was very different to that of the RPA, and the pace was much slower. Graeme determined to make the most of the opportunity to learn his trade well. Faced with the new career path of a surgeon, he set about the task of learning to tie knots and stitch up skin. True to character, Graeme did not dwell on his disappointment of being channelled into an unexpected career path. When not on duty he stayed with his elderly Aunt Varley and Uncle Perce in nearby Lindfield, where he spent his spare time sewing up bed sheets while holding the needle with forceps. If Graeme was destined to be a surgeon, he determined to be the very best surgeon he could become.

Graeme's time as senior resident at the Royal North Shore proved significant in several ways. A group of surgeons working there, led by Felix Rundle, had developed a specialised, interdisciplinary team that collaborated with physicians and nuclear physicists to achieve outstanding results in thyroid surgery. Graeme's observations of this team and how it worked would become important later in his own career when he would need to build his own specialised, inter-disciplinary team. Graeme was particularly concerned to make a good impression on this team and he had his chance when assisting Felix Rundle and Tom Reeve with a thyroid operation. When they discovered an unusual nodule and were pondering what it might be, Graeme recalled his studies and suggested it might be a rare kind of tumour called a Hürthle cell adenoma.

Graeme had the foresight to arrange a frozen section to be carried out and the answer came back fifteen minutes later: it was indeed a Hürthle cell adenoma. The team was clearly impressed with the young new resident and Rundle was prompted to blurt out: 'Clark, all your sins are forgiven.' But he then thought that might be too much encouragement for the young resident and modified his compliment to: 'Clark, some of your sins are forgiven.' For Graeme, of course, it was a reminder of the importance of thorough study and considering all the possibilities, however unlikely.

The other experience that was significant for Graeme was his time on secondment to Wollongong Hospital, where he 'saw life in the raw' and 'medicine at its best and its worst'. As a growing industrial centre, Wollongong had its share of social problems as well as industrial accidents. For the young resident working in the casualty department it meant that one night he might treat 'a young girl with venereal disease after a pack rape, and the next a man with 100 per cent burns from having fallen into boiling water at the BHP Steelworks'.[12] These were difficult and life-changing experiences for a young man barely out of his teens. Graeme's experiences at Wollongong made a lasting impact on him both as a surgeon and as a human being.

Interestingly, it was also in Wollongong that Graeme first drew the attention of the media as a surgeon—though not in the way he might have imagined. It was quite the news item in the local paper when he removed the appendix of a patient named Clark, in the Clark Operating Theatre, assisted by an anaesthetist named Clark.

At the end of the year, Graeme applied for a position as a tutor in anatomy at the University of Sydney. He felt this would help him hone his knowledge of the subject as part of his preparation for becoming a surgeon. Having been accepted for the position, he spent 1960 away from the hustle of hospital wards and back in academia. Again he made the most of the opportunity. In preparation for the surgical

41

exam required to become a Fellow of the Royal Australian College of Surgeons, Graeme's study group would toss small wrist bones into the air, and identify them before they were caught. What impact the *Human Tissue Act* later had on this practice is not clear, but Graeme's next venture in anatomical study is certainly no longer possible.

While studying the anatomy of the leg, Graeme fell upon the idea that it would be useful to have an actual human leg to work on. He went down to one of the city hospitals and enquired whether any amputations were planned for the day. He was in luck. The surgeon let Graeme have the leg, which he took home to Camden on the train and preserved in a drum of formalin. Because the container was too large to fit into any of the shelves in the laundry with the rest of his collection of body parts, he kept it under the house. If his father had been perplexed when years later he cleaned out the laundry, one can only imagine the anxiety caused by finding a human leg in a drum under the house.

The use of human body parts for the study of medicine has been rightly much better regulated in recent years. But it is still essential to the preparation of physicians and surgeons. Today, the idea of being able to purchase or obtain brains, legs and other body parts might strike us as being slightly medieval. Yet until very recently it was one of the best ways for dedicated young physicians and surgeons in training to learn their trade well before operating on living patients. While some of the situations created by taking 'study projects' home in those days created awkward and even humorous situations, surgeons such as Graeme Clark and others of his era were mindful of the respect due to all things human, and were grateful to those who donated their bodies to science so that they could become better healers of the living. Graeme still recalls that even amid the routine of working with so many bones and preserved tissues, he was always mindful that these had belonged to living humans who had been concerned enough to see medicine and science advance to be willing to donate their bodies for study. And thanks to the *Human Tissue Act* and better access to anatomy labs in medical schools, the elderly parents of physicians and surgeons, like Graeme's father Colin, are no longer left in the uncomfortable situation of having to explain what a severed leg might be doing in a vat under their house!

In the end, Graeme's study methods paid off, and he passed his surgical exams at the end of the year. In 1961 he was invited back to the Royal Prince Alfred Hospital—which had been unwilling to offer him a second-year general residency—as a registrar in brain surgery. While work in brain surgery was challenging, and proved very beneficial for his later work with cochlear implants, it wasn't where his heart was.

Three months later, when an opening became available at the same hospital for a registrar in ear, nose and throat surgery, Graeme applied for and got the position. Eight years after commencing medical studies, fifteen years after telling his pastor in Sunday school that he wanted to be an ear doctor, and nineteen years after telling his Year One teacher he wanted to fix ears when he grew up, Graeme Clark was finally fixing ears. Both Graeme and many who knew him well felt he had achieved his goal. In reality, his journey was only beginning.

CHAPTER 6

Student Christian Movement

An integral part of Graeme Clark's story of pioneer research into the bionic ear is also the story of his strong faith. It was often his faith that brought him both peace and a boldness to press forward when all the odds seemed against success. But Graeme's faith was not a mere remnant of a childhood upbringing in the church. It was instead something that came to him only through a series of experiences as an adult. The long journey of faith that became so critical for the path Graeme would follow began not so much in Sunday school, but in university, with his exposure to the Student Christian Movement.

For many up-and-coming professionals in the middle of the last century, the Student Christian Movement (SCM) played a significant role in the faith and values that would shape their lives and careers. This included students who went on to become some of Australia's most prominent scientists, including people like Professors Basil Hetzel and Charles Birch, who attended SCM meetings together as students at the University of Adelaide in the early 1940s. The reflections of Professor Hetzel (who developed iodised salt as a means of preventing serious intellectual birth defects—especially in the poorer countries of the world) on his involvement with the SCM and its influence on his life and career are typical of many of the era.

> It was the SCM that became my strongest extra-curricular interest over the three years before I became immersed as a senior clinical student . . . The SCM greatly enriched my life as a university student with long-term implications . . . [It] provided me with a general education and social contact similar to that gained in a university residential college. However, there was more than this—specifically, a Christian philosophy of life which has remained with me and inspired me.[13]

Formed in Melbourne in 1896 and dubbed by some as a 'university within a university', the SCM was initially a ministry of the Methodist Church in Australia. But it soon took on a broad, ecumenical dimension as it served the needs of a range of students looking for opportunities to reflect on their faith during their time at university. The organisation developed a reputation for encouraging activism and the discussion of ideas that many traditional Christians might find confronting. During much of the 1950s, when Graeme Clark was involved, the SCM was actually monitored closely by both the CIB (Commonwealth Investigations Branch) and ASIO (Australian Security Intelligence Organisation) due to its work with refugees from Europe, and the pacifism and conscientious objection advocated by some of its members. By the mid-1960s the group was involved in subverting the draft and supporting draft dodgers during the Vietnam War.[14]

For many, this is what the SCM was about. But it was also a place where intellectuals could discuss the implications for their faith of ideas arising from their fields of study. The SCM also provided the opportunity to challenge young people to consider their own personal faith.

How Graeme Clark came to be involved in the SCM is a fairly typical account. The profile of the organisation in the middle of the last century was such that anyone who had any contacts with the Christian community and was at one of Australia's universities could hardly escape regular invitations to attend SCM meetings or camps. At Scots College one of Graeme's favourite teachers, Barney Cubis, along with the school chaplain, Bruce Gentle, had already strongly encouraged Graeme to become involved with the SCM when he began university studies. Once at university, one of his good friends, Alick Hobbes, an active SCM member, invited Graeme to come along to meetings. These meetings generally took the form of lunchtime discussions on topics such as creation and evolution, determinism and issues of social justice. Looking back, Graeme felt the SCM experience was designed to make him and other students into good, mainstream liberal Christians. Some of those who attended SCM discussion groups were wary of belief in concepts like the miraculous. The God often spoken about was a force for good who was simply 'there', but didn't strike Graeme as being the sort of God who became actively involved in human affairs, let alone the lives of individuals.

Graeme was impressed, however, that many prominent, thinking people saw no contradiction between their faith and their science. This was nowhere more striking than in the person of Charles Birch, the Challis Professor of Biology at the University of Sydney and Graeme's first-year lecturer in zoology. Professor Birch by that time already had an international reputation and was one of the most prominent scientists in Australia. He was also one of the most popular lecturers at that time among the students at Sydney University. Yet here was a well-established scientist who had continued his involvement with the SCM beyond his own student days and was a regular speaker at SCM events in Sydney. Graeme was particularly taken by Birch's statement, made at an SCM meeting, that he 'wouldn't have become a Christian if not for the evangelicals, and would not have remained a Christian if not for the SCM'. In fact, it was through the faculty advisor to the SCM in Adelaide that Birch was introduced to the philosophy of Alfred North Whitehead, which so influenced his later philosophical and theological reflections.[15] For Graeme, the influence of the SCM in general, and Charles Birch in particular, helped him to see science and Christianity as a natural alliance.

If Birch came first to Christianity through the evangelicals, then to his mature faith through the SCM, the experience of Graeme Clark was somewhat different. He started out with the reasonable faith of liberal mainstream Christianity, and the evangelicals found him—in the Student Christian Movement. In those days it was quite common for the SCM to hold regular camps, and the question of personal faith was just as important at these events as issues of science and faith and social justice. At the end of Graeme's first year in medicine, just before embarking on his experiences of human dissection as a prosector, he attended an SCM camp at Otford, on the New South Wales south coast. The camp was in a quiet bush setting and the student leader was George Garnsey, whose father was the Anglican bishop of Sale in Victoria. At the end of the camp George, who was not himself part of the evangelical group, challenged those attending to consider their personal relationship with Jesus.

This was new language for Graeme. Up to that point his Christianity had been largely perfunctory and impersonal. His parents had encouraged Sunday school and church attendance, but had never pressured their children to believe in any particular tenets or express their faith in a certain way. Christianity and church were seen as good and positive influences in the Clark home, but there had always been a great deal of freedom for Graeme and his siblings Robin and Bruce to decide for themselves. The idea that he should, or even could, make such a personal decision about committing to Jesus was a new thought. In the end, the decision was not one borne out of any great sense of need to reform his life, nor out of a mystical 'Damascus Road' type experience, nor even the outcome of a prolonged intellectual struggle. Graeme simply thought to himself, 'What could it hurt?', and proceeded to say a quiet prayer. He didn't realise it at the time, but it was a turning point in his life. He recalls: 'I immediately had this powerful experience of peace and joy, which I thought was the presence of Christ.'[16] It would be some years, however, before the full force of this experience bore fruit in his life.

CHAPTER 7

Margaret

From an all-boy boarding school of the late 1940s to the male-dominated medical school environment of the early 1950s, Graeme Clark's opportunities to meet girls—even if his rigorous study schedule had allowed time—were limited. Fortunately, Graeme had a younger sister, Robin, who had no shortage of female friends. Two of these she invited home to Camden during a break from boarding school in Sydney. Graeme, who had, at just nineteen years of age, already managed to complete his first three years of medical school, was sent to meet Robin and her friends at the train station in Campbelltown and ferry them back home with their luggage. One of Robin's friends, fifteen-year-old Margaret Burtenshaw, caught Graeme's eye and he decided then and there that there was more to life than study. For Margaret's part, her first encounter with Graeme also made an impression. Graeme, she recalled, was wearing a brown sports coat, and had wavy hair. 'I clearly remembered his friendly smile as he came towards us along the platform. But I was embarrassed when he asked me if I had lead bricks in my bag!'[17]

Graeme may not have come up with the best ever first line to win over his sister's friend, but he did devise what he felt was a clever plan to get Margaret's attention, while at the same time demonstrating his sporting prowess. As a good host, he volunteered to take Robin and her friends for an afternoon of golf.

Teeing off on the first hole, Graeme put everything into a powerful drive for the flag. To his great embarrassment, he hooked the ball badly and went way off course. Fortunately, Margaret knew nothing of golf and remembers only being impressed at how far Graeme had hit the ball—and how much she enjoyed her first game of golf.

When Graeme discovered that Margaret had never played the game before, this gave him another idea, which at the time he thought highly original. He would offer to teach her how to swing the club, creating a great excuse to snuggle up to her while taking her through the swing technique. At this stage the romantic interest was entirely one way. Graeme remembers the snuggle—Margaret recalls only what a nice big brother Robin had, who was willing to show her how to hit the ball. With the mission to gain Margaret's attention apparently going nowhere, Graeme had one more trick up his sleeve—the direct approach, or at least what passed for the direct approach in 1954. Graeme sent Margaret a note via his sister inviting her out on a date.

Perhaps a movie or concert would have been the top choice of most young men in this situation, but Graeme chose to invite her to an orchid show being held at the Sydney Town Hall. The note, however, got her attention. This was her first date and she was quite excited. Graeme was delighted and not a little relieved when a positive reply came back. He now knew with some certainty that she was either interested in him, or very fond of orchids! As far as Margaret was concerned, she hadn't really given Graeme much thought after their time on the golf course. He was a nice young man, but was near to completing his third year of medical school and she was still in high school. She didn't consider him as a potential boyfriend until the note arrived via Robin.

Both Graeme and Margaret recall the date as a success, though neither could remember much about the orchids. They finished off the day by going to a local cinema to watch a newsreel about the first visit to Australia of Prince Philip and Queen Elizabeth II, who only two years earlier had ascended the throne. It is a reminder of just how very British Australia was in the 1950s.

Graeme and Margaret attended a few youth concerts together over the next couple of months, and Margaret met some of Graeme's friends from medical school. At this point the story of love at first sight might well have developed straight into 'they lived happily ever after'. But things happened rather differently. Graeme became busy with his studies, and was a bit self-conscious about dating a girl still in high school. Graeme and Margaret lost touch and continued on their separate ways. Graeme pressed on with his studies and his residency requirements, and found opportunities to meet other girls along the way.

Margaret finished high school and majored in English as part of the Arts program at Sydney University. Margaret's mother became very ill during her first year of study and this was a major blow. She took a semester off to help nurse her mother until her death in December of that year. This meant she needed to repeat her first year of university in 1957. By the end of her third year of university in 1959 she had become co-president of the Student Christian Movement in New South Wales and had secured an opportunity to do an honours year in English in 1960. She had long put behind her the brief high school romance with the handsome young medical student.

Margaret had, however, kept in touch with her old high school friend, Robin Clark. As Robin was now living in Sydney where she was studying pharmacy, Margaret decided to pay her a visit. Graeme, whom Margaret had not seen in over three years, also showed up unannounced at the same time to see his sister. So it came to be that Robin is able to take credit for introducing her brother to his future wife—twice!

Graeme had had little experience with dating and was convinced that it was important to 'play the field' and see what kind of suitable girls might be out there. What he realised the moment he saw Margaret again was that the field was very dull indeed, and that the most intelligent and attractive girl he had met so far had been the one he had dated first. After a hiatus of more than three years he determined not to let her slip away again. A few months later, on Margaret's twenty-first birthday, Graeme proposed and Margaret accepted. It was a fairytale courtship, but not of the usual sort. It had a beginning and it had an end—but no middle.

Graeme and Margaret were married on 27 December 1961 at Burwood Methodist Church. Three days later they set sail for Edinburgh. Graeme had been accepted to study surgery at the famous Royal College of Surgeons of Edinburgh. They travelled on the maiden voyage of the SS *Oriana*, the new flagship of the P&O line. Both felt it would be frugal to combine their travel to Edinburgh with their honeymoon. What they didn't plan on was a small berth below the waterline, which is all their budget could afford, or being woken early every morning for appearance at breakfast—and chided by the waiter if they were late. Their recurring bouts of seasickness were such that their memories of the Great Australian Bight and the Bay of Biscay include nothing of the views. Margaret and Graeme did, however, have very pleasant experiences visiting exotic cities such as Colombo, Cairo and Naples.

The honeymoon over, Graeme and Margaret arrived in Edinburgh in the midst of the Scottish winter. Graeme recalls:

We arrived in Edinburgh on a cold Sunday afternoon in winter, and found even the churches closed. The architecture was so different from Sydney's, and the city buildings had a sombre, black appearance from layers of ingrained soot. It emphasised how far we were from our families and friends.[18]

Graeme and Margaret knew they had to make the most of their new situation. They soon settled into life in Edinburgh with Margaret doing relief teaching to help support them. The Clarks also bought their first vehicle, an old Austin panel van with no heat, a driver's window that would not close, and questionable brakes. If Margaret had hoped that once Graeme returned home with his full surgical qualifications they would be driving much better vehicles, she was to be sadly disappointed. The old panel van with the window that would not close was, it turned out, a sign of things to come.

CHAPTER 8

UK studies

The time in the United Kingdom was the start of a new life together for the Clarks. It was also an opportunity for Graeme to hone his surgical skills in some of the leading centres of Great Britain. In the early 1960s most Australians still saw England as the mother country, and a chance for an Australian academic or medical doctor to further their training in the United Kingdom was highly prized. Graeme was determined to make the most of the opportunity.

The first stop for Graeme was the renowned Royal College of Surgeons of Edinburgh, which dated back to 1505 when the Barber Surgeons of the city were recognised as a craft guild. The following year they were granted a royal charter by King James IV of Scotland. Interestingly, the only entrance requirement for a prospective young surgeon at that time was that he be literate. By the time Graeme Clark arrived four and a half centuries later the bar had been raised considerably.

The Royal College of Surgeons is also renowned for its link with Lord Lister. Considered the father of modern surgery, Lister became a fellow of the college in 1843, and remained there for the rest of his distinguished career. Graeme was particularly inspired to be walking the halls where Lord Lister had done so much pioneering work. He would have had little reason to expect at the time that he would one day be a recipient of the Lister Medal, the most prestigious international award among surgeons.

For many hopeful medical graduates, studying at the Edinburgh Royal College of Surgeons and passing its exams meant not only qualification as a surgeon, but also the chance to put the prestigious 'FRCS (Edinburgh)' after their names. At the end of May 1962, after one semester at the college, Graeme passed his exams and was now officially a Fellow of the Royal College of Surgeons (Edinburgh).

To celebrate, he and Margaret took a belated 'real' honeymoon around Scotland and Ireland in their second-hand Austin panel van. Despite all their efforts at repair, the driver's side window still would not close. They brought along an Aladdin heater that they hoped would not only keep them warm but would also do for cooking. Unfortunately it went out at the slightest breeze and they were reduced to eating tins of cold sardines and vegetables. Nevertheless, this was a relatively relaxed and carefree time for the Clarks.

The FRCS in general surgery lived up to its reputation and helped Graeme gain a training position at the Royal National Throat, Nose and Ear Hospital in London. So, upon their return from this brief holiday, the Clarks packed their few belongings into their panel van and headed to London. In London, Graeme began the study of ENT (ear, nose and throat) surgery—taking him further towards his long-term dream of helping those with hearing difficulties—and Margaret was able to gain employment at a small private school in Wimbledon. They arrived in time for the winter of 1962–63, which was one of the coldest on record in England. Despite the freezing temperatures outside (and in their flat), it was a real treat to the young Australian couple who had only rarely seen snow. When the Thames froze they were able to join thousands of others walking and skating on the iconic river.

Graeme and Margaret had little money in those first years of marriage. They were a long way from home and family. And there was much work to be done. But these were happy years for the Clarks. For the time being, they had everything they wanted.

The motto of the Royal National Throat, Nose and Ear Hospital, taken from Mark 7:37: 'Audient surdi mutique loquentur' ('The deaf shall hear and the mute speak'), encouraged the young doctors coming through its doors to set their sights high. The challenge of the motto was certainly not lost on the newly qualified surgeon whose initial desire to help his father and others like him had set him on his medical journey. His dream of helping those with hearing loss appeared very much on track. Graeme was appointed as the senior house officer at what was simply called the Golden Square Hospital, which occupied an old building near Piccadilly Circus that was steeped in medical history. Before it was amalgamated with the Royal National Throat, Nose and Ear Hospital in 1942, the building had been the Hospital for Diseases of the Throat.

One of the stories Margaret remembers from their time in London is how Graeme very much wanted to get hold of a human temporal bone for his studies. Not having the same kind of contacts he did in Australia, this was proving difficult. The British, it seemed, were a bit more reluctant than the Australians at that time to give out human body parts to random medical students. So Graeme wrote home to his mother asking her to locate one he had left in his laboratory—otherwise known as the family laundry—and post it to him. Margaret remembers that when, a few weeks later, a package arrived from home, Graeme eagerly opened it. To his surprise, instead of the human temporal bone he had requested, he found inside a carefully wrapped sheep's skull. Attached to the skull was a note from his mother explaining it was the only bone she could find! The sheep's skull, which had travelled all the way from Australia via the post, occupied pride of place on the mantelpiece of their flat for the remainder of their time in London.

Graeme's most memorable experience from his time at the Golden Square Hospital came later that year, on Boxing Day. One of the patients had lost consciousness, and as Graeme had been a neurosurgical registrar in Sydney, he was able to diagnose the patient with a brain abscess from chronic middle ear disease. The situation required urgent action if the patient was to be saved. Graeme rang the hospital's consulting neurosurgeon who lived in the south of England. Heavy snowfalls at the time, however, meant that he was unable to travel to London. He was relieved to learn that Graeme had been a neurosurgical registrar. As he had no other choice, he left the matter in the young surgeon's hands. So it was that the newly minted general surgeon came to perform his first brain surgery. Graeme recalls his sense not only of great satisfaction but also of great relief when the patient recovered from surgery and regained consciousness. It was a huge boost to Graeme's confidence as a surgeon. But this proved to be an isolated experience. The Royal National Throat, Nose and Ear Hospital did not provide Graeme many challenges. Nor did it provide him with the kind of experience he most wanted—ear surgery.

Fortunately, another opportunity opened up and Graeme was appointed senior registrar to the well-regarded inner ear specialist Dr Jack Angel James of the Bristol Royal Infirmary. So Graeme and Margaret once more packed their meagre possessions into their panel van, and headed west, to Bristol.

As a surgeon, Graeme had one of his most memorable experiences in Bristol. While he was on duty, a farmer from Somerset was admitted with breathing distress and was blue in colour. Graeme had to act quickly to make a diagnosis. He inserted a mirror down the man's throat to see if anything was causing a blockage. He was shocked to find a large growth involving the voice box and the upper swallowing tube. Graeme was doubtful whether a tube could be inserted past the growth to administer anaesthetic and to allow for breathing. In case it was not possible, Graeme prepared to do a tracheotomy, which turned out to be necessary. Just as Graeme prepared to make the incision, events took a dramatic turn for the worse. Graeme recalls:

> To my horror, the patient's heart stopped. As he had a large barrel chest, it would have been impossible to do an external heart massage . . . I had no option but to open his chest and massage his heart. As I had assisted at many heart surgery operations, this wasn't a problem and his heart soon started again. I sent a message to the chest surgical registrar to sew up the chest and put an appropriate drain in place. The message came back that he wouldn't be able to do it for another two hours. So again, fortunately having done thoracic surgery, I just had to do the job myself. The patient recovered from his ordeal![19]

The incident taught Graeme how important all the various aspects of his training were. It also taught him that when an emergency arises, you cannot count on someone else being able to come in and take over. You have to be prepared to do the best you can in any given situation.

In Bristol Graeme not only gained some interesting surgical experience, but he also continued his studies to gain a qualification as an ear, nose and throat surgeon—though the results were not as positive as those of his surgical adventures. After a very busy weekend of clinical work, Graeme travelled to London to take the exam for the Diploma of Laryngology and Otology at the University of London. He had heard the exam was easy. It wasn't. He failed. It was not a familiar experience for Graeme. He had experienced nothing like this since his fourth-year medical school exams. Worse still, he failed because he didn't have enough anatomical knowledge of the inner ear.

Learning that the father of the bionic ear failed an anatomy exam on the inner ear is akin to learning that Einstein failed high school maths. It reminds us that the path to success in any field is not always straightforward, nor is it based on pure native talent or good fortune. It also teaches us that those who eventually succeed do not let failures, even embarrassing ones, stop them.

While all this was transpiring, Graeme had received an offer to work in an ear, nose and throat practice in Melbourne with Dr Russell Donald, a friend of his father. This was the same family friend who had recommended some decades earlier that Graeme's father buy the chemist shop in Stroud. Graeme and Margaret had already decided that it was time to return to Australia, and the position suited him. The only catch was that he still needed the surgical qualification in ear, nose and throat surgery, as at present he had only the general surgical qualification. The only available option was to sit the exam for ear, nose and throat surgery at the Royal College of Surgeons in London, which was a much more difficult exam than the one he had just failed.

Graeme passed the exam in London. But just in case he did not, he had also booked in to take another specialist surgical exam in Glasgow two weeks later. This presented complications, as Margaret was expecting their first child and the medical advice of the day was to avoid travel late in pregnancy. It was decided that she needed to head back to Australia before Graeme, so Margaret set off for Australia on the SS *Canberra*, while Graeme arranged to follow as ship's surgeon on a Shaw Savill merchant ship a couple of weeks later. Neither knew it then, but it would be nearly three months before Graeme and Margaret would be reunited.

CHAPTER 9

Ship's surgeon and Cairo castaway

In 1963 airline flights between the United Kingdom and Australia operated regularly. But Graeme Clark, the young surgeon and thoroughly modern man of science, had never flown. In fact, Graeme had a pronounced fear of setting foot on an aeroplane—leastways, as Graeme recalls, one that intended on leaving the ground. Hence he organised the more traditional, and longer, passage by ship. So while Margaret travelled home on the *Canberra*, Graeme arranged to follow a few weeks later. And what better way, he thought, for a young surgeon to travel affordably and in some degree of comfort, than by serving as ship's doctor? As the merchant ship on which he had organised passage slipped down the Thames and out of London, Graeme looked forward to an uneventful journey home to Australia.

That all changed as the ship steamed through the Bay of Biscay, and Graeme developed severe pains in his lower right abdomen. One did not have to be an Edinburgh-trained surgeon to recognise the unmistakable signs of acute appendicitis. Graeme was all too aware of the danger. A ruptured appendix could cause death within six hours!

He had seen this during his time as a registrar at the Royal Prince Alfred in Sydney. As these things happen from time to time at sea, most ships were prepared for such an emergency by arranging to have a ship's surgeon on board. Unfortunately for Graeme, that was him.

The prospect of removing his own appendix without aid of anaesthetic was daunting, to say the least. But as the pain worsened, it seemed that was precisely what he would have to do. He would need to use a series of mirrors to see what he was doing. And he would struggle to find a sterile environment. He would also need someone to assist. The only other person on board with any skill with a knife was the ship's bosun, or boatswain, who needed to be good with a knife for cutting ropes for rigging. Graeme began to prepare him for what to do so he could assist, and even finish, the operation should Graeme pass out. Graeme informed the captain of his situation and tried as best he could to endure the pain and hold out until the ship made port.

As the ship approached Port Said in Egypt at the upper end of the Suez Canal, the pain began to subside and a relieved Graeme, and we suspect an equally relieved ship's bosun, began to hope that it was not appendicitis and that surgery would not be necessary. Nevertheless, once they made port the captain ordered Graeme off the ship and into hospital. As captain he could overrule the medical advice of the ship's surgeon and was not willing to take the risk that the pain would flare up again, making the difficult and dangerous prospect of self-surgery necessary. A telegram was sent to Australia saying that Graeme was unwell and had been put off in Port Said. Then the ship, with most of Graeme's personal possessions still on board, steamed off down the Suez Canal and towards Australia without him.

Port Said was a thoroughly modern Egyptian city, which had only been established in 1859 during the construction of the Suez Canal. Standing at the northern entrance to the canal, the city became one of the busiest ports of the world. In fact, Rudyard Kipling once noted, 'If you truly wish to find someone you have known and who travels, there are two points on the globe you have but to sit and wait, sooner or later your man will come there: the docks of London and Port Said.' The sights and industry of Port Said were far from Graeme's mind, however, as he was put ashore. He needed medical attention in order to confirm that he did not have appendicitis.

The hospital to which Graeme was sent was a French Catholic hospital in the backstreets of the city. Graeme had only a small amount of schoolboy French to get him by. The surgeon there thought it probable he did not have appendicitis but wanted to operate to be safe. This would mean remaining at the hospital until the next ship arrived in two months' time. By now Graeme was starting to become quite worried about how and when he would get home to Australia and Margaret. To make matters worse, he had entered the country without disclosing his traveller's cheques, being under some stress at the time. He now realised what trouble he could be in if he tried to use these, as Colonel Nasser, the Egyptian president of the time, had decreed that any visitors not declaring traveller's cheques would be sent to prison. So Graeme effectively had no money to spend.

In desperation he did something he had never done before. He asked someone else for prayer. He had always before felt confident in his own abilities to get him through any situation. Now, for the first time, he realised he needed help. It was an unfamiliar experience for Graeme. He turned to one of the French nuns at the hospital and asked her to pray for him. The two of them went into the hospital chapel where she prayed in French and he in English. It was a significant moment for Graeme. Looking back, he recalls: 'For the first time I realised I couldn't rely on my own ability. It was a shock . . . Up to that point I was a very liberal Christian who didn't believe in miracles.'

The pain continued to subside and Graeme became increasingly confident that he was, in fact, not suffering appendicitis. So against the local surgeon's advice, he checked himself out of hospital. But now he had to get to Cairo and the British Embassy with no money. As it turned out, the same nun who had prayed so earnestly with him knew a Norwegian sailor with a broken leg who was travelling to Cairo that very day. She arranged an offer of a free ride, which Graeme eagerly accepted. He was beginning to think that God might actually be listening to his prayers.

Once dropped off in central Cairo, he had to locate the British Embassy. But he found the embassy had closed for the night and was completely dark inside. Graeme managed to find the Hilton Hotel, where he and Margaret had enjoyed lunch together two years earlier on their way to England. He asked the receptionist at the front desk if she knew the whereabouts of the Australian consular office. The receptionist thought for a moment, then said that while she did not know where the office was located, she did know where the Australian consul himself was at that very moment. He had just rung the desk and was at a function nearby. Would Graeme like to be put through to him? Indeed he would! To Graeme, this appeared as another in a string of happy coincidences since his session of prayer in the hospital chapel.

The Australian consul proved very helpful and was able to assist Graeme in finding a way to cash his traveller's cheques so he could purchase a plane ticket out of the country. Like it or not, Graeme was about to embark on his first aeroplane flight. He did not have enough funds for the trip to Australia, so instead had to book a flight back to London. Qantas was fully booked and the only plane available was a United Arab Airlines Comet.

At the time, several Comets had mysteriously exploded in midair and many people were wary of travelling on them; hence the available seats. Graeme was well aware of this, and it did not help to settle his nerves. To make matters worse, in a chance meeting with the pilot before the flight, he heard him complain to an official that the plane had not been properly serviced. It was not the best of circumstances for a first flight for someone with a fear of flying. But Graeme was desperate by this stage to get out of Egypt and find a way home to Australia. The flight proved uneventful and Graeme soon found himself back in London with a new sense that God really did answer prayer. As he later recalled, 'These experiences were just the start of a change in my attitude of self-reliance to one of waiting on God in prayer. This was to become a necessity later when it came to developing the bionic ear.'[20]

This growing spiritual awareness, which would become such a vital part of Graeme's life and a mainstay through the many challenges and obstacles to come, was further enhanced when he arrived in London. Graeme needed to find a qualified doctor to confirm whether or not he had appendicitis. He contacted Geoff Shead at the London Hospital, who had been a friend from his student days. Geoff was able to put Graeme's mind at ease that he was not suffering from appendicitis, but most likely from a 'spastic colon'. More than that, however, Geoff was an active Christian and was able to help Graeme explore what he had experienced during his time praying with the French nun. He was also able to talk to Graeme about his new sense of a God whom he not only now understood he needed, but whom he also now believed was listening. While waiting to return to Australia, Graeme spent a great deal of time with Geoff and his wife praying and reading the Bible.

After Graeme's teenage conversion experience at the Student Christian Movement camp, he had sought to learn more about what it meant to have faith. As a young academic he turned quite naturally to the most recognised Christian scholars of the day. He read widely in the writings of the liberal German scholars Rudolf Bultmann and Paul Tillich. Yet their approach to the Christian faith did little to inspire him, and his interest soon waned. Now, however, he was experiencing a whole different approach to Christian faith, and it was striking a deep chord within him.

When Graeme was finally able to get on the Dutch steamship the *Willem Ruys* bound for Australia, he met up with Dr Bill Hawes, an English missionary doctor on his way to Borneo. A great deal more time on board was spent praying and discussing the Bible and matters of faith. By the time Graeme finally arrived in Sydney he was a very different person to the one who had first set out more than ten weeks earlier. The faith that had been largely background music in his childhood, and an intellectual discussion point during his medical school days, had become more real. Graeme Clark, the liberal and cultural Christian, had become Graeme Clark, the man of personal faith. And faith, as it turned out, was something he was going to need a very good measure of on the journey to come.

CHAPTER 10

Resettling in Australia

The return to Australia was followed by much activity. Graeme and Margaret's first child, Sonya Dorothy, was born on 29 March 1964 at Epworth Hospital in Melbourne, just three months after Graeme had rejoined Margaret. A little over a year later the Clark family was further extended with the birth of their second daughter, Cecily Anne, who was born on 25 August 1965, also in Melbourne. With a rapidly growing family and a new career, life had become very different for the Clarks, both professionally and personally.

During this period Graeme not only had to learn the basics of helping Margaret to care for their young children, but he also had to busy himself getting established in the medical practice with Doctors Russell and Gwen Donald. In those days the Donalds were a rare husband and wife medical team. They had a growing practice located on Collins Street, Melbourne, which focused on allergy patients. But they were in need of a surgeon to work with them. This meant Graeme's main task was to work with those patients who needed nose or sinus surgery. Graeme's early work as an ear, nose and throat (ENT) specialist in Melbourne had a strong focus on plastic surgery of the nose, helping people to look better and breathe more freely.

But Graeme missed being able to work with ears. So, in addition to his other duties, he put his hand up to do three days of work per week at the main teaching hospitals in the city. This meant Graeme was often rushing, with a bag full of surgical implements in one hand and a sandwich in the other, from one Melbourne hospital to another.

He found the work very demanding and tiring. He attended the public hospital clinics at least three days each week, namely the Austin Hospital, the Alfred Hospital, the Repatriation General Hospital, and the Royal Victorian Eye and Ear Hospital, the latter of which would play an important role in his future career. He then had two days to do his share of the work in the practice, which he was asked to buy into. As the junior partner, it meant he travelled around Melbourne to different hospitals doing most of the surgery for the practice.

Graeme began at this time to rediscover 'the fire in the belly' for research, especially in the area of hearing loss. He remembers having had a few profoundly deaf people visit him at the Eye and Ear, and his sadness at having to turn them away because there was nothing that could be done for them. He then began experimenting with ultrasound as a treatment for an inner ear condition called Ménière's disease, which caused hearing loss and issues with balance. And he became quite enthusiastic about performing a new stapedectomy operation to correct middle ear deafness. Graeme was supporting his family with his nose reconstruction work, which he took very seriously. He saw it not only as a way to help people, but also as an art. He was also continuing to stay involved with his first passion, ears, whenever he could. The hundreds of basic throat and nose operations were becoming routine. And they were also putting a strain on the old high jump injury to his neck. All the hours required looking up patients' noses and down throats were taking a toll. He knew something had to change.

He turned to God, as he had learned to do in Port Said, Egypt, and asked for healing. But the pain only increased to the point that Graeme could no longer continue his surgical practice. Like many who pray earnestly, he wondered why God did not answer his prayer. The solution to his problem, after all, seemed obvious. The worsening pain in his neck, however, led him to consider other career paths.

If he abandoned clinical practice for research, he wondered, what would be his area of focus? Could he still find a way to pursue his long-held dream of helping those like his father with severe hearing loss? Towards the end of 1966 Graeme, who by now was the head of a clinic at the Eye and Ear, was having lunch at a park opposite the Royal Melbourne Hospital between surgical procedures performed as part of his private practice. He had picked up a medical journal to read during his lunchbreak. The journal was the July 1966 issue of *Archives of Otolaryngology*. Perhaps not everyone's first choice for a lunchtime read, but it changed the course of Graeme's career, as well as medical history. Graeme's attention was drawn to an article by Stanford University professor of medicine Blair Simmons. It was titled 'Electrical stimulation of the auditory nerve in man'.

Remarkably, Professor Simmons had conducted experiments on several human patients in 1964 in which a six-channel device was brought into contact with the hearing nerves, producing electrical stimulation. While the patients were not able to comprehend complex speech-like sounds, they were able to detect sound and even observe a range of pitches. The discovery of the Blair Simmons article led Graeme into a whole new world of highly speculative and contentious research, mostly led by French researchers up to that time, to stimulate hearing electrically in the deaf. It was a watershed moment in Graeme's thinking. The challenge, as he saw it, was to do the impossible. Finding a way to correct nerve deafness would satisfy the fire in his belly that had not let him find peace in his private practice. He had found his life's calling.

The die was cast. Graeme made his decision to turn his efforts to medical research. He wrote to Sir John Eccles, a Nobel laureate in neurophysiology whose Boyer Lectures of 1965 had impressed him greatly. He asked his advice about taking up physiological research and, as Sir John was an active Catholic, also about his Christian faith. Sir John replied that at thirty years of age, Graeme was already too old to embark on such a new course. Fortunately, Graeme ignored the advice. He recounted this years later to Sir John's daughter at a dinner party they were both attending. She replied, 'I am glad you did not take my father's advice—I never did!'

Graeme made contact with one of his old professors from Sydney, Peter Bishop, who in turn put him in touch with Professor Colin Dunlop, who was the first university researcher in hearing and brain science in Australia. Graeme was accepted into the University of Sydney to work with Professor Dunlop, where he undertook a study of how the brain codes sound and how it might be possible to restore hearing in deaf people by the use of electrical stimulation of the hearing pathways in the brain.[21] Graeme had reached another turning point in his journey towards his pioneering contribution to bionics. It meant also that the family's sojourn in Melbourne was over. They would be heading to Sydney, familiar ground to both Graeme and Margaret.

For Graeme, PhD studies in Sydney were the opportunity to thoroughly follow up on the research of Blair Simmons, which he had discovered only a few months earlier, and all related research into the electronic stimulation of the hearing nerves. He was well aware that if he told Professor Dunlop what he actually had in mind—to eventually develop an implant that would stimulate the hearing nerves and allow the successful coding of speech—he would think he was mad. But a PhD thesis examining all the work previously done on this preposterous idea would seem harmless enough to be acceptable. It would provide Graeme the opportunity to meticulously determine what was already known about this area, as well as what obstacles would need to be overcome. While his thesis supervisor saw his student working on an interesting piece of research in brain physiology, Graeme was laying out the foundations of a future research and development program with far-reaching consequences.

To say that Graeme was entirely focused on his research may be something of an understatement. Margaret recalls one occasion during Graeme's PhD work when he failed to return home for the evening. As he often became caught up in his studies and remained at university long after everyone else went home, she did not panic. She fed the girls, put some food aside for Graeme, then put the girls to bed. But then midnight came and went, and there was still no sign of Graeme. In those days there were no mobile phones, so she had no way of contacting him. As the wee hours of the morning wore on, she became increasingly concerned for her husband. At 4 a.m. she finally called the police. They located Graeme at his desk at the university, working blissfully away, completely unaware of the time.

While the grand plans about restoring hearing for the deaf were formulating in Graeme's mind—and often keeping him up through the night—there were also pressing practical matters for the Clarks to concern themselves with. Graeme, at age thirty and with a wife and two daughters, had left a well-paying clinical practice in Melbourne to return again to the life of a student in Sydney. Problems with transportation and meeting the needs of the family were further challenged, though happily so, when a little over a year after their arrival in Sydney, Margaret gave birth to their third daughter, Roslyn Lucy, on 10 August 1968.

Transport, housing and finding the money for day-to-day expenses were all going to be a stretch. Graeme and Margaret found housing in Sydney very expensive. Fortunately they were helped by a friend to find a somewhat run-down but affordable two-bedroom flat in Cremorne. It may not have been much, but the location was convenient. They felt they had all they needed. Graeme later recalled, 'To become poor again was in some ways a wonderful relief as I was no longer in the rat race where colleagues compared earnings and possessions.'[22]

And when, soon after the move to Sydney, the old Vauxhall they had been given by Graeme's parents broke down in Gundagai on a trip back to Melbourne, the Clarks found there simply wasn't the money to replace it, even with another second-hand vehicle. Again, Graeme found a positive side to the apparent inconvenience. Being forced to take public transport everywhere, Graeme discovered a certain kind of freedom in the new simplicity and routine of his life. He recalls: 'While waiting for public transport I had time to think about research. This was a new and exciting experience. To be playing about with ideas that one might be able to test later in the research laboratory was what I wanted to do.' Where others would have seen inconvenience and disadvantage in such circumstances, Graeme, predictably, saw opportunity.

CHAPTER 11

Australia's youngest professor of medicine

Graeme soon discovered during his PhD studies in Sydney that he had a natural passion and aptitude for research. He was not content with fiddling around the edges of the possible, merely tinkering with what was already known. He had a desire to break new ground, to take big research risks in the hope that he could make a significant difference in the lives of the profoundly deaf. Yet the return to academic study was not without its challenges.

When Graeme arrived in Sydney with his family in early 1967 he soon began to discover just what he had let himself in for with his return to studies. He remembers:

> I spent the next three months reading auditory physiology literature and learning what all these totally new areas meant. It was really a totally new and different discipline. What was a post stimulus time histogram? What was the structure of the auditory nervous system? How was it studied? Here were people steeped in the area of visual physiology who had spent the greater part of their lives working at it. My training

in medicine had not prepared me for this. Medicine had given me the confidence to think I could easily know about all matters biological. But in effect I knew very little about the area. I was excited by the challenge and also a little daunted. But I knew I had to master it if I wanted to prepare myself for experimental work on electrical stimulation of the auditory pathways.[23]

Graeme commenced a series of studies at Sydney University in 1967 in which he used electrical stimulation on animals to determine how best to design a cochlear implant for humans. In late 1969 he completed his PhD thesis on the topic, 'The middle ear and neural mechanisms in hearing and the management of deafness'. The letter from the university confirming the thesis had been accepted and all requirements for the degree met did not arrive until 29 December of that year. Graeme was beginning to wonder if the academic administrators had gone off on summer holidays and forgotten about him. After choosing a highly specialised and controversial research path over private surgical practice, the question for Graeme now became, 'Where to next?' Now that Graeme had his PhD and had developed research skills to match his medical and surgical credentials he needed to find a position that would allow him to put these skills together and continue his research. As had become his custom, he prayed and he waited.

When he saw a notice advertising the position for chair of a new Department of Otolaryngology (Ear, Nose and Throat) at the University of Melbourne it looked like an ideal opportunity to pursue his vision. It was to be the first chair in the field of otolaryngology in the southern hemisphere. Graeme knew he was too young and inexperienced by at least a decade. He also knew his prayers would be best formulated by asking that God's will be done. So with this prayer, he sent off his application.

Graeme's PhD thesis had been completed (though not yet formally accepted) just as the position was advertised. Graeme was technically eligible for the role, although it was a long shot. The department would be small, but its head, carrying the status of professor, would have significant influence in gaining grants as well as the freedom to pursue specific research projects. The department was to be based out of the century-old Royal Victorian Eye and Ear Hospital in East Melbourne, where Graeme had done clinical work only a few years earlier. In the hospital where he was recently known as a young practitioner, he was now seeking to return as head of a new research department with professorial standing.

The position, the William Gibson Chair of Otolaryngology, had a decade-long history behind its establishment. Peter Howson CBE, who was instrumental in seeing the chair established, remembers that it was his colleague Dr Ken Howsan, the medical director of the Eye and Ear, who complained to him in 1959 that there was a great deal of difficulty getting registrars in ENT at the Eye and Ear due to the many changes taking place in the field. The idea born of this conversation was that a professorship in otolaryngology could be established in conjunction with the University of Melbourne to meet this need. This project occupied Peter Howson throughout the 1960s. The Royal Melbourne Hospital (RMH), where most of the chairs in medicine were located, was also interested in having the chair located there, and it was not at all certain it would be based at the Eye and Ear. There would have been advantages in being located within the context of other medical and surgical chairs at the RMH, but, as it turned out, the independence and freedom that was provided by being a part of the Eye and Ear was precisely what Graeme Clark would need to pursue the bionic ear project in earnest.

The Royal Victorian Eye and Ear Hospital already housed the University of Melbourne Department of Ophthalmology, founded in

1963 under inaugural Professor Gerry Crock. Originally named the Melbourne Institution for Diseases of the Eye and Ear, the hospital was founded in 1863 at the end of the gold rush period by the Irish physician Andrew Sexton Gray. Gray was originally from Limerick and had trained as an eye and ear surgeon in Dublin, and also worked as assistant to Oscar Wilde's father before migrating to Australia. Gray was concerned to find in Melbourne so many poor, especially among miners and their families, who had eye and ear diseases but could not afford help. His institute was founded as only a single-bed infirmary, but grew quickly. Two years later, in 1865, he treated 2060 patients, and in 1873 he merged his hospital—by then known as the Melbourne Institution for Diseases of the Eye and Ear—with the Ophthalmic and Orthopodic Institution founded by English-trained eye doctor Aubrey Bowen to form the Royal Victorian Eye and Ear Hospital. After several moves around the eastern side of Melbourne, the hospital settled at its present location in 1881. Such was Gray's influence that many consider him the father of Australian ophthalmology. And the hospital he founded continued to grow in both size and reputation. As Melbourne's third oldest hospital, and with a long history of specialisation, the links it developed with the University of Melbourne as a teaching hospital in the 1960s and '70s were not surprising.

As the University of Melbourne was preparing to add another teaching department at the Eye and Ear, it found itself in something of a race with the University of Sydney to see who would be the first to establish a department of otolaryngology within Australia. George Swinburne, who was the senior ENT specialist at the Royal Melbourne Hospital, had worked very hard to promote the establishment of a chair in Melbourne, while Sir George Halliday, who was the prime mover behind the foundation of the Oto-Laryngological Society of Australia and one of its early presidents, was pushing for the establishment of a similar chair in Sydney. A big advantage for Melbourne was that they already had a specialised eye and ear hospital and a chair in eye surgery, thus paving the way for a similar chair in ENT. As it turned out, it took Sydney an additional ten years to get their department. By that time the University of Melbourne's Department of Otolaryngology, under the leadership of Graeme Clark, had already made international headlines with its first cochlear implants.

In 1961 the drivers of the proposed chair were challenged to raise £100,000 for its establishment. By 1964, £95,000 had been raised for the new chair, so they confidently went back to the university heads, thinking they had nearly reached their goal. To their great disappointment they were informed that in the three years it had taken to get to that point, the cost of establishing a new chair had gone up to £150,000. It took another six years of fundraising, planning and negotiations before permission was finally granted to advertise the new chair position.

One of the early supporters of the chair, George Swinburne, was known to be interested in being appointed the inaugural professor. Sadly, George passed away in 1969, leaving the field wide open. Graeme Clark, in Sydney, was not fully aware of this history at the time. He knew only that a position ideally suited to him and his vision had been created, but that he was likely too young and inexperienced to get it. He did, however, have the encouragement of Gerry Crock, the professor of eye surgery at the Eye and Ear Hospital who had also been appointed at a young age. Graeme felt his application should at least merit consideration.

The selection committee narrowed the search down to three candidates: a UK applicant, a local clinician, and the young surgeon recently appointed as head of an ENT clinic at the Eye and Ear, now a freshly baked PhD living in Sydney, Graeme Clark. By October they had narrowed the search down further to just two applicants, one of whom was Clark. Graeme had made the short list for this pioneering new position in part because of his strong focus on research. At the time the University of Melbourne Faculty of Medicine, under the leadership of Sir Sydney Sunderland, had a reputation as a research-oriented faculty. This was distinct from the model found elsewhere at the time, especially in the United States, where heads of departments of medicine were successful clinicians in private practice. They were expected to bring their expertise into the university while remaining active in private clinical practice. A further appealing feature of Graeme's application was his interest in pursuing research in the area of the electrical stimulation of the auditory nerve, which he had already been doing in Sydney. This was bold, but it got the committee's attention.

The committee wanted evidence of research interest and ability. Remarkably, Graeme was never called down from Sydney for an interview. Instead he was asked to send in a copy of his recent Master of Surgery thesis on the structural support of the nose, his recently submitted (but not yet accepted) PhD thesis on research on the electrical stimulation of the inner ear, and a major statement on how he would run the new department if offered the position. The committee found itself split, with two in favour of the more experienced candidate and two in favour of giving Clark the position. That left Peter Howson, the chair and fifth member of the committee, to make the decisive speech, indicating his preference. Against all odds, Howson found himself favouring Clark, who he felt was 'much more dedicated and less interested in private practice'. As he later recalled, he told the committee that they had a 'choice between a clinician who would have been very good if we had wanted to go down that path and a chap who was dedicated to research and teaching rather than the clinical side'.[24] After his speech the committee agreed unanimously to offer the position to Graeme Clark.

Graeme received a phone call from a university official at lunchtime on 27 October 1969 offering him the new chair of otolaryngology. He could hardly believe his good fortune. The position could not have been more suited to his plans for developing a cochlear implant. At thirty-four, Graeme Clark became the youngest professor of medicine then serving in Australia. To celebrate, he and Margaret splurged, despite their tight budget, and went out to dinner at the new Centrepoint Tower revolving restaurant in the Sydney city centre.

Intriguingly, the funding for the position began on 1 January that coming year, but the facilities were not yet built—indeed, they had not yet even been designed. Graeme was offered the opportunity to come at a later date but opted to begin right away. So it was that Graeme, Margaret and their three daughters packed their belongings once more and drove to Melbourne over the Christmas break, allowing Graeme to show up for work at the Eye and Ear on 2 January 1970. By the end of that year, Graeme would not only have a new job to attend to, but also another daughter, with Merran Rose Amelia born on 7 November 1970. The growing Clark family now had four daughters.

Early in Graeme's tenure as the William Gibson Professor of Otolaryngology, a welcome dinner was held in honour of the new professor. The speaker at the dinner was George Gray, president of the Society of Otolaryngology. Both George and the society had been actively involved in promoting the establishment of the new department. The tradition at these dinners was for the speaker to find some embarrassing anecdotes, glaring blunders or some half-forgotten scandal concerning the new appointee to help put them in their place. So George put his team to work to search through Graeme's records, talk to colleagues, and dig up some interesting dirt. They came back to him empty-handed, which was unusual. At the dinner George let everyone know that his team had done their best, then turned to

Graeme: 'Clark, you are either extraordinarily clean, or are very good at covering your tracks!'

A chequered past, however, was not all Graeme was lacking as he took up his new role. With no facilities for the new department, the hospital had to be creative in finding space for Graeme and his staff. This was particularly difficult, as a wing of the hospital was being built and its current facilities were spread over several buildings. Graeme's offices and small team were housed in various unused parts of the Eye and Ear. And his laboratory was located in an old morgue in a separate building. Here was another situation that many would have seen as disadvantageous, but which Graeme welcomed as an opportunity. Graeme was offered the opportunity to design one whole floor of the new Peter Howson wing of the Eye and Ear to suit the needs of his department. With the help of his friend, Sydney-based Danish architect John Andersen, Graeme was able to design the new facilities to suit his specific needs, including his planned research into cochlear implants.

Maud Gibson, in honour of whose father the chair had been named, donated a further $15,000 to help develop the facilities. But much more was needed. Graeme turned to Sir Henry Bolte, the longstanding premier of Victoria, to provide funding to complete the facilities. Graeme had been forewarned that when he went to Sir Henry's office, he may well be expected to have a number of drinks with the premier. Indeed, Graeme found that he was expected to match the premier's ability to down glasses of whisky. Several glasses later, Graeme had his promise of funding. Unfortunately by that stage Graeme, who was not a serious drinker, realised that he was too drunk to make it home. He found a quiet spot at the bottom of a stairwell where he spent a couple of hours sobering up. It was the only time he can recall ever being intoxicated. Graeme recovered from his ordeal, the funds were given for the renovations, and Sir Henry himself officially opened the new department in 1972.

While the path may have seemed long and complex, Graeme could not have written a better script for pursuing his vision to restore hearing to the deaf. He would no longer have to seek permission from department heads, or work with laboratories and facilities designed for other types of research. The remaining obstacle, and it proved to be a big one, was how to fund the level of research that would be required to see the project through to successful completion. More whisky-drinking sessions with the Victorian premier, Graeme concluded, were not an option.

CHAPTER 12

Reginald Ansett and the Channel 10 telethons

There is a perception in the community that medical doctors and academics are all financially well-off, and that research, especially research in medicine, is very well funded—or at least that this used to be the case. With Graeme not only a practising surgeon, but now also a professor of medicine, many might have thought the Clarks would have had few financial cares—either personally or professionally. The reality was very different on both counts.

Graeme and Margaret had made great sacrifices so that Graeme could pursue further studies in preparation for a career in research. Their growing family meant not only additional expenses, but also that Margaret was, quite happily as she recalls, a stay-at-home mother during these years. In was not until the 1980s that she would return for a time to her teaching career. So Graeme and Margaret, despite the couple of years spent in clinical practice, were in many respects a typical young family starting out, with Graeme only recently having completed the final phase of his formal studies.

When Graeme first began his duties as professor of otolaryngology in Melbourne, he wore a second-hand suit to work every day, and still recalls being asked by colleagues why he always wore the same ties. He smiled and said simply they were his favourites. The reality, however, was that he owned just the two. The frugality of those days could be seen most poignantly, however, in the family's mode of transport. When the Clarks and their daughters moved back to Melbourne, they drove down in an old Rambler which they had purchased from a colleague, George Berci, who was at that time in the process of pioneering endoscopic surgery. The car used as much oil as petrol, but they had little choice other than to keep it going. Graeme took public transport to work in the early years in Melbourne and saved the car for family use.

After the Rambler, the Clarks bought a second-hand Rover. But the rear doors wouldn't shut properly and tended to come open when the car was moving. With four young daughters in the back this was clearly not acceptable. To solve the problem Graeme ran a rope over the roof of the car, slid it through the rear windows which were opened a crack on each side, and tied it tight. It created a bit of a draft in winter, but it kept the doors from swinging open. Worse than the draft, however, the girls—three of whom were now at school—found it very embarrassing. They kept a close watch out and would yell 'Duck!' whenever they saw anyone they knew, so that none of their friends would see them in a car that had to be held together with rope.

Graeme's contract with the university allowed him the right of private practice alongside his academic work. This was very common at the time and was a good source of additional income for many academics. Graeme never fully took up this right. There were times in those early years when the additional income would have been very welcome. But Graeme did not want to sacrifice time that he could otherwise give to establishing the new department and pursuing his research objectives—particularly work on what he later named 'the bionic ear'.

If things were tight personally, managing the budget of a new department was even more challenging. With no established funding sources and no track record in research, funding had to be found for researchers, lecturers, laboratory equipment and other expenses.

As Peter Howson recalled, the committee knew that if they appointed Graeme they would have to help him find funding. But they had already found obtaining the money to support the new chair to be a long and difficult process. In the department's first three years most of the money came from the hospital budget with little outside help. The dean of the medical school, Sydney Sunderland, said that Graeme could have $6000. The rest he would have to raise through his own efforts. It didn't help that criticisms were circulating among many scientists and ENT specialists that a cochlear implant just wouldn't work, and that the university was throwing money down the drain on the project.

The normal way forward for a promising research project at the time was to seek government grant money. While Graeme had some initial success, he soon found that this source had all but dried up. Many of his Australian colleagues either believed that the task was impossible, or that the Americans were so much better funded that they would get there first. It seemed that these sceptical colleagues were often well represented on boards and panels of key funding groups. Hence, time and again the various government granting agencies were convinced that they should not risk money on Graeme's research.

To get any grants at all, Graeme and his team found they had to disguise their research requests so it looked like they were studying something other than the electrical stimulation of the auditory senses. Even getting the money for a computer took two years! At that time a Hewlett-Packard computer with 8 kilobytes of memory cost $30,000.

This was a great sum of money for a computer with less processing power than the average mobile phone today. Yet without it the work could not progress. The computer, considered a dinosaur by today's standards, was state of the art at the time. Once obtained, it was used to develop the first speech processor program for the first cochlear implant. It is now, literally, in a museum.

Graeme also did his part with a great deal of door-knocking and public speaking, with some small successes. In fact, the sight of Graeme at fundraising lunches and other such events became so commonplace around Melbourne that one of his research students drew a cartoon of him shaking a tin on the corner of Collins and Swanston streets, raising funding for the bionic ear project.[25] In fact Graeme missed few opportunities to raise money for the project. During a visit to his dentist to have a tooth pulled in 1973 he was asked how work was going. Graeme proceeded to explain what he was trying to accomplish and the difficulties of financing the research. Not only was the tooth removal successful, but his dentist rallied his Lions Club to raise $7000 for Graeme to employ another research assistant.

Graeme had known from the beginning that developing a bionic ear was going to be very expensive. He wrote: 'So I proceeded to pray and at the same time to speak at Apex, Lions and Rotary luncheons, raising about $200 from each engagement. This went on for months and I could see I would be ready to retire before I had enough money.'[26]

But the luncheons paid off in an unexpected way. The Australian Broadcasting Commission (ABC) ran a story on its national evening television news about Graeme receiving a $2000 donation from the Apex Club in Melbourne for the project. Watching the program that night was Sir Reginald Ansett, founder of Ansett Airways and owner of Channel 10 (then Channel 0). As it happened, Sir Reginald's daughters had a friend who was deaf, so he was very much aware of the difficulties experienced by those with hearing loss. He asked his medical officer to ring Dr Jean Littlejohn, a prominent former chief ENT surgeon at the Eye and Ear. When she vouched for Graeme's enthusiasm and ability, Sir Reginald rang Graeme with the offer to run a telethon on his television station to help raise the needed funds.

Telethons, a concept now largely unknown to younger generations, were a mainstay of fundraising in the 1970s. Commercial television stations seeking to show their support for the community would often work with a major charity or a specific project to raise money via a television special. For several hours, between various entertainment pieces, information would be given on the project for which money was being raised, and the public would be informed why it was important. Telephone operators took calls at the station and graphs would be shown regularly to update viewers on how much money had been pledged towards the project. Not all the money pledged ever came in, but a substantial amount generally did. If a project could get a telethon behind it, it not only gave direct access to a very large pool of potential donors, but it raised the profile of the project substantially, making other fundraising efforts easier.

So began a series of three telethons in the mid-1970s that provided a large portion of the money needed to carry the project forward. In preparing for the initial telethon it was pointed out to Graeme that raising funds for a 'multi-channel cochlear implant' might be a little hard to sell to the general public. Could he come up with a catchier name? Graeme suggested, 'how about calling it a "bionic ear"', as the term bionics was well known from the popular television series of the day, *The Six Million Dollar Man*. The producers liked the idea and the name stuck.

That initial telethon, held in October 1974, was a huge success. Although the Channel 7 telethon which had raised money for the Melbourne Royal Children's Hospital earlier in the year had been much bigger, the $87,233 raised by Channel 10 for the bionic ear project was the largest single funding amount Graeme had received up to that time. As Graeme noted, 'the money was enough to pay for an engineer, a computer programmer, a technical officer, electronics parts and some other equipment'[27] with a little money left over to help cover the salaries of existing staff.

The expenses associated with the research necessary to ensure the success of the project remained significant. Graeme soon calculated that he would be out of funding by the end of that year, 1975. He had kept Sir Reginald up to date on the research's progress, and hoped that he might be able to persuade him to hold another telethon. Sir Reginald proved a committed supporter. He scheduled two more telethons, one for 16 December of that year, and another one in May of 1976. As Graeme believed, at this stage, that the first implant of a bionic ear should be able to take place in late 1976, this seemed likely to be enough to get the project across the line. Even though the public had now already generously given to two previous appeals, the telethon of May 1976 was the most successful yet, raising $125,888.

The telethons not only produced much needed funding, they also galvanised public support for the research. The nature of telethons was such that they tended to draw in a wide range of people to the project. Many of Graeme's staff became directly involved and this only served to strengthen their own sense of commitment to the bionic ear project. Even Graeme's family joined in. Margaret went around Eltham with a tin collecting donations. And the Clarks' oldest daughter, Sonya, who was in the later years of primary school during the telethons, still has vivid memories of going to the television station for filming, and even going out onto the street with her dad to 'shake a tin'.

The way in which the fundraising developed meant that Graeme not only had the money needed to further the work, but now also had an incredible amount of publicity about the project. He soon found, however, that this had drawbacks as well as benefits. It was now much easier to gain funding from other sources as his project had become 'high profile'. There was growing recognition within the community of the value of his research. On the negative side, some of his colleagues did not appreciate all the attention Graeme and his project were receiving. And there were now heightened expectations within the community and especially the media that his project would produce results—and soon.

CHAPTER 13

Imagining the impossible

In 1964—nearly six years before Graeme Clark took up the new professorship in otolaryngology at the University of Melbourne— Professor Merle Lawrence in the United States, one of the world's leading hearing scientists, declared: 'Direct stimulation of the auditory nerve fibres with resultant perception of speech is not feasible.'[28] His comments came after a surprisingly long history, dating back to the end of the eighteenth century, of efforts to do just that. When Lawrence surveyed the many early and recent attempts to electrically stimulate the hearing nerves so that speech could actually be perceived, he saw nothing to give him any hope for success. He finally declared the entire enterprise an impossibility. Yet this is precisely what Graeme Clark was proposing to do. What was it that Graeme saw in the history of this failed venture that others had missed? What gave him such a strong conviction that success was more than a slim possibility?

Remarkably, the Italian scientist Count Alessandro Volta, from whom we get the term 'volts', had already experimented with electrical stimulation of hearing at the end of the eighteenth century. His Italian colleague Luigi Galvani had discovered, quite by accident ten years earlier, that electrical current could stimulate movements in the legs of a dead frog. It was the kind of early science that inspired Mary Shelley, just a few years after Galvani and Volta's experiments, to write the story of Dr Victor Frankenstein. While Shelley wrote her novel as a horror story, many have come to see the work as the first true science fiction story, replete with the fear that tampering with nature may lead to unexpected and dreadful results. Volta was in many ways a prototype of Victor Frankenstein. He could not resist the temptation to discover what else might be stimulated by electrical current. He concluded that there was only one way to find out. He reported the results of his experiment in a paper delivered in 1800 to the Royal Society in London. In it he described how he introduced rods made of thirty to forty pairs of silver and zinc compounds into his own ears, connected them to an early version of a battery, and turned on the switch. Wrote Volta:

> I pushed deep into each ear a metal rod with a rounded end and I had the other two ends making contact with my apparatus [battery]. At the moment when the circuit was thus complete I received a jolt in my head; and a few moments later I began to be conscious of a sound, or rather a noise in my ears.[29]

Clearly this was a man committed to his science. What Count Volta heard was a continuous crackling or bubbling sound during the time the apparatus was connected that sounded to him like 'some dough or thick stuff was boiling'. Critics suggested it was the sound of his own brain starting to boil. Others, including eventually Graeme Clark, came to believe that Volta was actually the first person to produce an electric stimulation of the hearing nerves. It is incredible when we think of it. Before the invention of electric toasters, electric motors, even electric lights, scientists had already used electrical current to stimulate the auditory nerves.

Volta never repeated the experiment as the jolt he received when he first switched on the electrical current frightened him and he concluded that it 'might be dangerous'.[30] Nevertheless, from this time it was known that electrical stimulation could produce the apparent sensation of sound. It was a huge leap, however, to think that this might not only be done safely and practically, but that any such sensation of sound might correspond to sound waves produced in the environment, let alone those produced by human speech.

The whole idea that electricity could stimulate hearing sat relatively dormant after this extraordinarily early start, until the latter half of the nineteenth century. Progress in the scientific understanding of electromagnetism and electric circuit design, advances considered by Graeme Clark in his PhD thesis, led to new possibilities for picking up the earlier experiments of Count Volta. In fact, what Graeme undertook in his doctoral thesis at Sydney University was nothing less than a thorough review of all that had been discovered about the electrical stimulation of hearing since Volta's early experiment. A summary of his findings on the history of this research was later published in his article 'Cochlear Implants: Historical perspectives', in *Profound Deafness and Speech Communication*, edited by Geoff Plant and Karl-Erik Spens and published in 1995. Graeme's findings, while perhaps obscure for those outside the history of science, are important for understanding what gave him hope and indeed the confidence that the deaf could hear again through electric stimulation of the auditory nerves. So just what did Graeme discover?

Graeme learned, for instance, that in 1855 the pioneer French neurologist Guillaume-Benjamin-Amand Duchenne of Boulogne achieved the stimulation of the auditory senses by inserting a vibrator into a circuit which contained a condenser and induction coil. Unlike

Volta, Duchenne had the good sense to run his electrical current into other people's heads—which allowed him the luxury of repeat experiments. Using alternating current, what he achieved was reported as a sound resembling 'the beating of a fly's wings between a pane of glass and a curtain'. Similar experiments were further repeated in 1868 by the German neurologist and expert in electrotherapy, Rudolf Brenner. What was unknown, however, was just what caused this phenomenon.

Two Russians, G.V. Gershuni and A.A. Volokhov of the Military Medical Academy in Leningrad, were able to show in 1936 that it was the cochlea itself that was the site of the stimulation which was producing the sensation of sound.[31] This research was further reinforced and refined by S.S. Stevens and R.C. Jones in 1939 and 1940. They found that the sensation of sound could be produced when the middle ear acted as a transducer and also when electrical energy was transmitted into sound by a direct effect on the basilar membrane. Most of these experiments, however, were conducted on people with full hearing. Significantly, Stevens and Jones also found that a hearing sensation, though a very crude one, could be produced in patients with minimal or no hearing through a direct electrical stimulation of the auditory nerve. The ground now seemed set for a major breakthrough in this research, and a number of researchers in the 1950s and '60s took up the challenge. Yet the breakthrough did not come.

In 1950, J. Lundberg became the first person to directly stimulate the auditory nerve. He used sinusoidal current for the procedure which he conducted during a neurosurgical operation, but reported that the patient could only hear noise. A more thorough experiment was conducted in 1957 by the French team of otologist Andre Djourno and physicist Charles Eyriès. They placed electrodes directly on the auditory nerve of a patient being operated on for cholesteatoma. The patient was able to distinguish differences in pitch and, remarkably, was also able to distinguish a few simple words such as 'papa' and 'mama'.

Similar results to those of Djourno and Eyriès were achieved in 1964 by a team led by Blair Simmons who stimulated the auditory nerve of a patient undergoing surgery for a cerebral ependymona. One of the findings of Simmons' team was that the placement of the electrodes on the auditory nerve was crucial for the results. Also in 1964, a team led by James Doyle superimposed speech signals using an electrode placed outside the cochlea. His patients were able to perceive rhythm of both speech and music and to distinguish the occasional word. Blair Simmons continued his work in this field, conducting more extensive studies in 1965 and 1966 in which six electrodes were implanted into the cochlea of a deaf patient. His patient was able to detect change of pitch. The patient was also able to recognise when speech patterns were being transmitted but could not discern their meaning. It was Simmons' article reporting the results of these later experiments that proved pivotal in the career of Graeme Clark. William House, working in this period with John and James Doyle, also did similar work from 1961. But their results were only reported in 1976.

By the time Graeme Clark committed to the project, much was already known and a number of significant strides had been made. As Veronica Bondarew and Peter Seligman put it, 'the invention of the cochlear implant is a muddy story'. This was not so much because of any dispute about who contributed what, but simply because there were so many strands to the story and so many parallel lines of development taking place. They explain:

> The question of who invented [the system of the cochlear implant] can be divided into single-channel and multi-channel devices, although

even here, the division is rather blurred. The origin of the single-channel system is relatively straightforward. It was invented by the French. Regarding who invented the multi-channel cochlear implant, it is necessary to rephrase the question and ask who developed the first multi-channel (as distinct from multi-electrode) cochlear (as distinct from auditory) prosthesis. There appears to be no clear answer to this question, but it was probably also the French.[32]

The French had been active in the field very early, with Djourno and Eyriès making the first attempt at a clinical single-channel implant as early as 1957. Unfortunately a dispute between the two over a broken electrode in two successive patients, for which Eyriès blamed Djourno, led to the end of collaboration between two of the most successful researchers to date on the electrical stimulation of the auditory nerve. While Djourno continued his research, he never achieved the same level of success as when he had worked with Eyriès. Djourno also refused to work with an industry partner for fear that commerce would taint science, which further limited his ability to continue his research. He was finally able to implant a device in a third patient, a seventeen-year-old Vietnamese woman in 1958. But she returned to Vietnam after six months and all opportunity for follow-up was lost. Before her return to Vietnam, however, it was found that she was able to detect sound. Although she could not distinguish words, she reported that she found the device helpful for lip-reading by highlighting the rhythm of speech. But with no industry partner, two failed devices, and a third patient disappearing overseas, the venture came to an end and the French lost their promising lead in the field.[33]

While all this effort proved unsuccessful in helping deaf people to hear, it did lead to the hope that this eventually might be possible, even though Professor Lawrence, as noted earlier, declared in 1964 that this was not feasible. One of those who was inspired by these studies, and who disagreed with the negative assessment made by Lawrence and others, was the young Australian researcher Graeme Clark.

For Graeme, this part of his journey began that day in late 1966 when he happened to take Simmons' journal article with him into the park to read during lunch. It was this report of findings from experiments in 1965 and 1966 that alerted Graeme to the potential for the electric stimulation of the auditory senses. Graeme was excited to read how a profoundly deaf patient had actually been able to hear sounds, even though he was not able to understand any speech patterns. As Graeme recalled, 'That initial report was enough to fire me up. I felt this was my mission in life. It was clear from the article that there was still much to learn before profoundly deaf people might be able to understand speech.'[34]

Graeme's doctoral studies convinced him that implants that would allow the deaf to distinguish speech were not only possible, but possible within the very near future. Hence when he was appointed to the inaugural chair of otolaryngology at the University of Melbourne at the beginning of 1970 he took the dramatic step of issuing a press release that many, including Professor Colin Dunlop, his doctoral supervisor from Sydney, thought was completely irresponsible. Graeme announced in the *Daily Telegraph* of 23 January 1970 that it was his goal to develop a cochlear implant that would allow the deaf to hear and that he thought this would be possible within ten years. It was a prediction that proved to be remarkably accurate.

Where others looking at the intensive research of the past two decades saw only dead ends, Graeme saw the potential, even the inevitability, of a breakthrough. Many saw a public declaration of intent regarding such a seemingly illusory goal as foolhardy. But Clark achieved two things thereby. Firstly, he began a relationship with the public via the media that would prove vital in gaining the support and funding the project needed. Secondly, he had committed himself in the most public way possible to achieving the biggest breakthrough for the profoundly deaf since the Abbé Charles-Michel de l'Epée developed sign language at the Paris Deaf School two hundred years earlier. For Clark, there was now no turning back.

CHAPTER 14

'That clown, Clark'

Today anyone who was even remotely associated with the development of the cochlear implant developed by Graeme Clark and his team wears it as a badge of honour and pride. After all, the achievement is widely recognised as one of the greatest success stories of Australian medical science. But in the 1970s, before the success of that first implant, things were very different.

Medical science, like many other fields, is highly competitive. The image of scientists in related fields from different universities and nations working together to produce life-changing breakthroughs is often more myth than reality. There is often fierce competition between nations, universities, departments and individual scientists for limited funding. In many cases there are close races to see who can make and report a major breakthrough first. Those who are successful, and who gain publicity in the process, are virtually guaranteed further funding.

Now imagine you are a researcher in the medical sciences in Australia in the 1970s, competing for a very limited pool of funding.

Suddenly a young unknown researcher announces that within ten years he believes he can do the impossible—help the deaf to hear through a multi-electrode, multi-channel cochlear implant. It is something some of the best researchers in America and Europe have tried and failed to achieve for decades, and have largely declared impossible. But the idea generates great public interest. Telethons are even held to raise money. Of course, given all this attention and funding going towards what is clearly impossible and a complete waste of time, the project is going to draw some very strong opposition. Such was the environment that Graeme Clark, Australia's youngest professor of medicine, found himself in from the very beginning of his audacious venture.

From the moment of Clark's announcement in January 1970 of his bold intention to use his role as founding professor of the University of Melbourne's Department of Otolaryngology to develop a cochlear implant for the deaf, he encountered incredulity and resistance. His 'doctor father' from the University of Sydney, Professor Colin Dunlop, sent Clark a copy of the *Daily Telegraph* report with the bold predictions in the press report highlighted, noting his concerns that making such predictions, especially for such an improbable project, was foolhardy. Dunlop let Clark know that he was very concerned about the rash claims he was making about bringing hearing to the deaf. He could not understand how Clark could make statements that his breakthrough would be as exciting as heart transplants.[35] And this was an example of friendly fire!

Other criticisms were less friendly. It was argued that the idea was a waste of money, dangerous to the patients, would benefit very few in any event, would at best be an aid to lip-reading. On and on the torrent of concerns went. Graeme was not finding the Australian medical and scientific community particularly encouraging for a nation known for its 'can do' attitude. Some were simply dismissive without having even clearly considered the concept. Graeme recalls that one ENT surgeon dismissed the whole idea, claiming that it was on a par with pushing a light bulb into a particular body cavity and turning on the electricity.

One of his fellow professors of medicine at Melbourne, who had argued that a department of otolaryngology was unnecessary and represented only a minor speciality, remained vocal in meetings about the young upstart professor. Graeme recalls this particular professor at one meeting actually stating that since it was well known that Clark's tenure was limited, there was no point in his putting forward any long-term proposals. Graeme, understandably, found the comments upsetting. He wondered what this professor knew that he did not. Were there indeed no long-range plans for continuing his position? Graeme felt he had to gain reassurance from the university hierarchy that his department was not a short-term experiment. Once satisfied that this was not the case, and that the university was committed to the department, Graeme had to respond to these vocal comments that were clearly designed to undermine both his confidence and his credibility. He did this in the only way he knew: he redoubled his efforts to succeed with the development of a cochlear implant.

Yet the internal opposition continued. As one observer commented, Graeme 'was neither fish nor fowl. He was not a pure scientist and neither was he an applied surgeon'.[36] So his colleagues, who didn't quite know how to classify Graeme, complained regularly to the vice-chancellor of the university, Sir David Derham, that Graeme was wasting his time (and the university's money) on experimental work that would lead nowhere.[37]

Years later Graeme sat down to reflect on the difficulties of those days with Peter Howson, who had been not only foundational to the development of the department and Graeme's appointment as the first professor, but had also been the chair of one of the research committees of the Eye and Ear hospital in those early years. Graeme brought up with Peter his own recollections of one of his key colleagues being very critical of his research.

'Yes,' Peter recalled. 'He was more or less saying the thing will never work. And there were also many of the seniors at the Eye and Ear who were also very critical.'

'I don't think,' said Graeme, 'anyone was in favour of it. I felt for you, Peter. You not only had to go around and support this project, but you also had to defend this bloke Clark who was not the normal expected appointee for such a position.'

'The real problem we encountered,' said Peter, 'was with the research. "Why give more funds to this when it is just pouring more money down the drain? It will never work and it is just a waste of time." And this is the response we got research committee meeting after research committee meeting.'[38]

Graeme had to dig deep within himself to find the motivation to persevere. In order to have any chance at success he had to be prepared to sacrifice the ideal of either being a pure teacher, or a pure researcher. He had to get 'excited by neurophysiology, then engineering. Worse still, he practised the surgery, and even worse, tried to get money'.[39] His colleagues felt it was professional folly, a career-ending dead end. But Clark simply continued to pray for patience, and to recall a lesson he had learned many years before as a youth reading about Louis Pasteur. Pasteur, he recalled, did not get caught up in making a false dichotomy between pure and applied research. For Pasteur there were only two kinds of research: good and bad. Graeme was determined, whatever anyone else thought, to do good research. As he put it, 'I was determined to do good science and base the clinical work on this alone. And it was not to be done other than very rigorously.'

By 1980, after two successful implants and the publication of results in various media, including a film showing the tests conducted on Rod Saunders, there was still a significant amount of scepticism within the scientific community. Experts in the field still had trouble believing that the device really worked and that it was safe. At one conference a leading ear surgeon asked, 'What is that clown Clark doing putting multiple electrodes in the inner ear?'[40] Clearly, there was still a long way to go.

Among some of the opposition Graeme received in his early years was the derogatory designation as the 'cat doctor'. Initially it was a way of dismissing his research because of its association with hearing experiments conducted using cats. By the end of the process, however, the use of animals for research into the cochlear implants itself became controversial and a source of opposition for the work.

When Graeme Clark first began serious experimental research into the electrical stimulation of the hearing nerves while undertaking doctoral research at the University of Sydney, he was introduced to animal experimentation. Even before the use of animals in experiments began to be an issue of significant public concern, Graeme was very much aware of the need to treat any animals used as humanely as possible, and to do no more experimentation than necessary.

It was at the University of Sydney that he was introduced to the use of cats as an ideal animal for research into hearing. When he took up his role at the University of Melbourne, the old morgue at the Eye and Ear became what some referred to as the 'cattery' because of the use of cats for the research needed. Again, while there was still little public sensitivity about such research, Graeme was keen to treat the animals well, including introducing what he called regularly scheduled 'play time' where the cats could get out of their cages, interact and run around. Given that there was no way to provide the benefit to humans without this research, Graeme accepted that it was the only way forward. Interestingly, while he was at the University of Sydney, cats had been provided to researchers, but Graeme now found that he and his students were responsible for catching their own. So it was that he became aware of most of the seafood processing shops around the city, which had a problem with stray cats and were happy for university medical school students to come out and remove them.

The use of animals in research became a significant issue for Graeme and his team when they received a contract for research into implants in children from the US National Institutes of Health in the mid-1980s that required the use of macaque monkeys. An article appeared in the local paper about this and a good deal of negative publicity within the community was generated. When it was explained to reporters that cats and not monkeys were ordinarily used, this helped little, as many people had cats for pets. After this episode, and despite the best possible treatment of the animals, Graeme decided to do as much as possible further necessary animal testing using rats. When it was pointed out that rats were as sentient as cats, Graeme agreed, but then wryly observed: 'But for some reason, people are not as fond of rats.' But he well understood the point. Graeme knew there was no way to achieve some medical breakthroughs for humans without prior testing on animals. He was heartened when the Melbourne-based ethicist and animal rights advocate Peter Singer, who had been sought out for comment on the use of the macaque monkeys, agreed that in cases where a significant benefit for human beings could be achieved and there was no other alternative, then a limited use of animals for experimentation was acceptable.[41]

CHAPTER 15

Assembling the team

When Graeme Clark took time to reflect on the development of the cochlear implant in 2000, by which time the device was recognised as an undisputed scientific, medical and commercial success, he knew it was a journey he could never have completed alone. He found it somewhat embarrassing when people not familiar with scientific work assumed he had somehow single-handedly developed the bionic ear. He wanted to give credit to the many specialists in medicine, surgery, audiology, engineering, electronics and other fields who had, at one time or another over the previous quarter of a century, served as part of his research team.

Of course, it is in Graeme Clark's nature to be thorough. It was, after all, his thoroughness and absolute refusal to take any shortcuts that allowed him and his team to achieve what many had said was impossible. When Graeme began to list all those specialists in so many interrelated fields who could proudly count themselves as part of his team, he began with the obvious colleagues. Those there from the early years, the heads of groups, the people who played key roles in significant breakthroughs, the departmental secretaries—all had played vital and necessary roles. But still, he knew that these achievements would in turn have been impossible without all the graduate students and research associates working as a part of these overall teams. So Graeme began to go through his memories and check through his records—concerned that no one was left off the list of those to be thanked in his book, *Sounds from Silence*. In the end he settled for a list of 208 names which, he added, could have been longer.[42]

But who were these people—and how did Graeme find them? In the beginning, the research section of the new Department of Otolaryngology ran on 'the smell of fumes from an oily rag'. Certainly no other professor in Australia at that time was known to go out to busy street corners with a donation tin to raise the money needed to keep his staff. Early on, Graeme recognised that one of the best and most affordable sources of help would come in the form of graduate students who needed to work on projects that dovetailed with their thesis topics.

One of the lessons he had learned during his time at Sydney University was that research students, especially in the field of medicine, did excellent work and they cost little, if any, money. As an additional bonus, these graduate students served as points of contact with their co-supervisors in various other departments, who in turn represented a wide range of specialities.[43] While this meant that Graeme's team was younger and less experienced than many research teams of the time, they more than made up for this with their energy, enthusiasm and willingness to attempt the impossible.

The first on board in 1970 were: Cynthia Russell (née Kent) (secretary), Sue Rubenstein (part-time secretary) and Rodney Walkerden (senior technical officer). They were joined in 1971 by Kim Berner (research assistant), John Delahunty (surgeon), Howard Kranz (research student in psychology), Don McMahon (surgeon), Harry Minas (research student), John Nathar (research student), Field Rickards (research student), David Scrimgeour (research student), Joe Tong (mechanical engineer) and John Vorrath (surgeon). These were the first of the 208 who would contribute directly to the bionic ear project by the turn of the century. As many were graduate students, there was a tendency to move on after a year or two. Others—like Joe Tong, who began when he was a graduate student in mechanical engineering, and Field Rickards, who began as a research student and went on to become a professor of education of the hearing impaired—remained to work with the project for more than two decades.

Not only was Graeme no ordinary researcher, but he was also no ordinary supervisor. Graeme did not come to the job with a great deal of experience leading teams. It was another skill he had to learn. He found the time spent in management, and dealing with the sometimes difficult egos of so many talented people, exhausting. Yet Graeme cared about his team members as people and worked with them collegially. He often stayed with them long into the night when they were in the midst of an experiment or seemed on the verge of significant progress.

His research students remember Graeme as being open to their ideas. Rather than insist that everyone follow his own line of thought, he welcomed innovation. When engineer Peter Seligman, for instance, suggested that the technology was available to reduce the large computer system needed to process the information gathered by 'the gold box' into a processor that could actually be carried about like a small briefcase, Graeme encouraged him to see just how small he could make such a device. The result, of course, meant that implant recipients did not have to come to a special room at the Department of Otolaryngology filled with a bank of computers just to hold a conversation. The device could now work anywhere the recipient went.

The fact that so many of Clark's team went on to achieve significant success in their respective fields is testimony not only to the quality of individuals Graeme was able to attract to his project, but also the kind of encouragement he gave the members of his team and the vital lessons they learned in working on the bionic ear project.

CHAPTER 16

The gold box

By the time Professor Clark had begun to assemble a competent team around him, the theory behind his research project was beginning to gain credibility. Electrical stimulation of the auditory nerves in the inner ear could and did produce sensations of sound, and there was evidence that some distinctions between sounds were possible. But to produce something that allowed actual speech to be distinguished was going to take not just some surgical finesse and a deep understanding of neuroscience and speech, it was also going to require a very great and probably very expensive amount of technology. At the centre of this technology was something Clark's team began to refer to as the 'gold box'.

By the end of 1973 Graeme had demonstrated in the experimental animals the limitations of achieving effective speech coding via electrical stimulation using a single electrode to convey speech frequencies. The question was then whether a multiple-electrode implant would work where the single-electrode option, favoured by many of his predecessors and competitors, had failed. The only way to settle the question was to construct a multi-electrode cochlear implant. This implant came to be known as the 'gold box'. What was in this box would be critical to the success of the whole enterprise.

Graeme produced a video for a 'mini-telethon' that ran on Channel 10 (0) in late 1973 explaining how this sealed gold box would work and what his team planned to put in it.[44] It would be a challenging engineering feat, to say the least. Graeme was very fortunate that Dr David Dewhurst, a physicist who was also one of the country's leading electronic engineers, was watching the program and became excited by what he saw. Dewhurst thought, here is something I could invest my energies in that is not simply going to make someone money, but is going to truly make a difference in people's lives. He rang Graeme the next day and asked for a meeting. It didn't take much persuasion for Graeme to convince Dewhurst to join the team.

The challenge that Dewhurst and his team of engineers faced to develop what Graeme needed was immense. They had to create a sealed box that would receive information from outside, eliminating the problem of infection. This box would also need to contain a very large number of circuits. Graeme wanted the electronics to allow the team to explore physiological concepts for speech processing and formant-based ones. In the end, this meant a gold box that could contain 6000 separate transistors. Only the recent development of the silicon chip made this feasible. In fact, had the team been doing their work only two years earlier, the technology to achieve the miniaturisation necessary for an implantable gold box would not have existed.

The second major telethon in 1975 provided enough funds to hire an engineer. Jim Patrick was chosen by Graeme from a select group of applicants. With Dewhurst at its head, Graeme's team of engineers was falling into place.

An interesting aside to this unusual (for a department of medicine) collection of engineers and computer scientists was that during the mid-1970s the Department of Otolaryngology was the second largest purchaser of electronic components within the entire university. Graeme recalls that he often wondered in those days what the university accountants must have thought was going on in the Ear, Nose and Throat Department!

But even with so many top-flight engineers on hand there were still many problems to be solved. Without an effective gold box there would be no bionic ear. The team needed to determine how to transmit information through the skin to the sealed implant (gold box); whether the gold box would have an internal or external power source; the exact placement of the implant in relation to the ear; the design of the electronics within the gold box; the packaging of these electronics; and whether a backup connector would be necessary.

The team worked on solutions to many problems through 1975 and 1976, including while Graeme was away in England on sabbatical studying speech perception. When Graeme and his family arrived back in Melbourne in May 1976 he saw how much work remained to be done and how naïve he had been to think the first surgery could take place later that year. He recalled, 'I hadn't learned that in electronics, circuits don't perform to expectations and faults develop in components.'[45]

With much hard work, a benchtop version of the circuit design was finally completed by the end of 1976 and was ready for testing. But this version was large scale, taking up approximately one square metre of circuitry board. It was certainly not something that could be surgically implanted behind a patient's ear. The challenge was to reduce this circuit design down to something that would fit on a silicon chip. For this Graeme was much indebted to Jim Patrick and Ian Forster, who were able to integrate the circuit design onto a Mastermos silicon chip—an early silicon chip that had predesigned units that could be connected together, thus making it more affordable.

The process, however, was not an easy one, and Graeme notes that 'we lost eighteen months in the race with researchers in San Francisco, Paris and Vienna'.[46] But Graeme needn't have worried. The overseas teams were having their own difficulties. And those who took apparently easier options were continuing to fall short of the goal. There was, it turned out, no shortcut. The gold box had to be right if any significant result was to be achieved. All the careful research and testing into multi-electrode versus single electrode, sealed versus unsealed, power source and circuit design upon which Graeme insisted—even though it slowed the work of the team—turned out to be absolutely necessary.

CHAPTER 17

Life at Eltham and Kiama

Soon after Graeme took up the chair in otolaryngology the family settled in Eltham, on what was then the eastern fringe of suburban Melbourne, along the Yarra River. Initially they rented in the area while building a home which they were able to move into in 1972. Today, Eltham is a somewhat exclusive neighbourhood that redefines the concept of 'leafy' suburb. It has an abundance of mansions and grand estates, many with a tennis court and swimming pool at the rear, set neatly behind tree-lined drives and well-manicured lawns. But in the early 1970s Eltham was a very different place, and this is still reflected in a few homes like the Clarks'—a single-storey mud-brick house set within an acre of bush grounds. When the Clarks built there, it was a rural area too far out from Melbourne to attract the big homes. It was a community known more for 'alternative living' than stately manors. For the bushwalking, pottery-turning and eco-conscious Clarks, it was the ideal location. The peace and nearness to nature that Graeme recalled from his childhood, and knew he would need in order to endure the stress of the venture he was undertaking, were to be found there. The Clarks worked with architect and mud-brick home builder Alistair Knox to design an environmentally friendly home that would blend as much as possible into its surroundings.

The Clarks moved into their new home in 1972 with daughters Sonya (eight), Cecily (six), Roslyn (three), and Merran (one). Despite all the successes and accolades that were to follow in Graeme's career, the Clarks resisted all temptations to add a pool, a second storey, an English garden, or any of the other usual trappings of success. They had a comfortable family home with a pottery kiln at the back, views to the Yarra River and plenty of native vegetation and animal life, and room for the children to grow and play. Their second daughter Cecily fondly remembers celebrating Earth Day each year at the home of Alistair Knox, their architect, and his wife Margot, who was an artist. They would spend the day making bread and candles and doing other earth-friendly activities. There may have been no pool at the Clark home, but there were bonfires, birds, native scrub and plenty of visitors. For daughter Roslyn, what stood out was bike rides on quiet unsealed roads, camping in the backyard, tyre swings, canoeing the rapids of the Yarra, and keeping a goat named Zinkie. Why would the Clarks want anything more?

There was certainly no pretence about the family. By the time their youngest, Jonathan—who was born the year after the first successful implant operation—went to high school, he quickly became aware that he was the only one who lived on a dirt road in a mud-brick house, or whose parents drove a fifteen-year-old Peugeot Familiale.

For Graeme, the home at Eltham and his family were his retreat from the world of high-pressure science, the endless chasing after funding, and holding at bay a seemingly endless queue of critics. In response to the question of how he coped with the pressure of so much opposition to his research, during an interview with George Negus, Graeme responded: 'I chose a very peaceful place in Eltham to live, which made an enormous difference. I made a point of actually growing up with the kids. I made my hobby, in the weekends, to play with them, to share with them. Instead of going to the golf course, I went to the backyard with the kids.'[47]

Margaret, for her part, between juggling duties as a mum to four young daughters, found time to complete a Diploma in Education. Until this time she had the Bachelor of Arts (Honours) in English and no formal teaching degree. This enabled her, when the children were older, to pursue her vocation of teaching. As she was considering where she might teach, Margaret heard of a new school, Donvale Christian, which had been built out among what, at that time, were still the scrub and orchards of Donvale. While considering what to do, she was reading her Bible and came suddenly across the verse 'Go out into the wilderness and help them'. She took this as a sign and went to Donvale to teach English, where she remained for most of the next decade. Her time with Graeme in England in the 1960s had been a great adventure for an English major. She had long looked forward to making use of those experiences from the heartland of English literature in the classroom. Finally, she had her opportunity, and she enjoyed the role.

Margaret's efforts, however, at getting Graeme to read the classics proved something of a challenge. When he read for pleasure, he sought motivation. At one stage in the mid-1970s, when many thought what he was attempting to do was impossible, Graeme confided to Margaret that he was only interested in reading miracle stories, because that was what he needed to believe in. He did, however, take great encouragement in reading Alexander Solzhenitsyn's *One Day in the Life of Ivan Denisovich* and *Cancer Ward*. He could relate to the struggles portrayed in these stories. It helped him put into perspective the opposition he received in his pursuit of a bionic ear.

For holidays the family went each summer to Kiama, 120 kilometres south of Sydney in the Illawarra region, where they had a small holiday house. Photos from family holidays show a relaxed and bearded Graeme Clark, with longish hair and floral patterned shirt, and often a surfboard close at hand. Those who encountered Graeme with his family at the various beaches near Kiama would never have picked him for one of Australia's leading medical researchers.

Kiama is a coastal town built upon ancient volcanic flows that made the region very rich for wheat and dairy farmers. In the 1970s, remnants of a rainforest which once covered the whole area still stood in isolated patches, such as the Minnamurra Rainforest. The rainforests, old quarries, idyllic beaches for swimming and surfing, walking trails, art and craft shops, local fishing villages and lighthouses (especially the Kiama lighthouse on Blowhole Point), all made the area popular for summer holidays, with the population of the main centre, Kiama, tripling during weeks after Christmas.

For the Clarks, who were keen cyclists, bushwalkers, surfers and connoisseurs of local arts and crafts, Kiama was an ideal escape from the pressures of research and the stresses of the city. It was to Kiama that the Clarks would retreat every summer, and meet up with Graeme's parents and the families of his sister, Robin, and his brother, Bruce. The growing clan would converge on the Clarks' three-bedroom holiday cottage with their tents and caravans in such a migration that Graeme felt the neighbours must surely have breathed a great sigh of relief when January came to an end and the Clarks vacated Kiama for another year.

For Graeme, driven by his dedication to restore hearing to the deaf, holidays at Kiama were not only a time to refresh, but also to think about his research. He recalls:

It was a time to be recreated physically and also spiritually. I bought a surfboard and for a while tried to keep up with the younger generation, but I soon turned to boogie boards and body surfing. There was time, too, just to sit and think about research. It might be after a walk at Minnamurra Falls, on the headland after a swim, or on the beach while the children played at the edge of the surf. I filled notebooks with research ideas and plans for their execution for the following year.[48]

We should not imagine, however, that the multi-talented professor from Melbourne was able to accomplish great feats of surfing, hiking and swimming, all the while thinking through pressing research problems. In fact, Graeme, who loved the beach and swimming, was not actually a strong swimmer. Swimming was the one merit badge he was not able to achieve as a boy scout. So it came to be on one occasion that Graeme went for a swim at Kiama beach while being a little too preoccupied with thoughts of research. So preoccupied, in fact, that he did not notice just how far out he had swum, or just how big the waves, called dumpers, had become. Once realising his predicament he had no choice but to put his hand up, calling for help. A surf lifesaver on duty had to paddle out on his board, attach a rescue belt around Graeme, and tow him back into shore. The enthusiastic but inexperienced lifesaver, however, didn't look back once Graeme was attached, and dragged him so often under water that Graeme feared he was going to be drowned in the process of being rescued. Graeme made a note of the fact that the beach could be a dangerous place and that he should reserve his most intense thinking for dry land.

CHAPTER 18

Study leave in England 1975-76

When the time came for Graeme's first sabbatical from his role at the University of Melbourne, he was at a critical point in his work on the bionic ear. He had surrounded himself with a high quality, multidisciplinary team. He had also been reasonably successful, especially through the Channel 10 telethons, in raising enough funds to ensure the continued progress of the research. His own journey of study and research had taken him from anatomy, to surgery, to neuroscience, to engineering. But he had become increasingly aware that there was still one big piece of the puzzle missing. If he was to lead the project to a successful outcome, he would need a thorough understanding of how speech actually worked. Graeme was particularly aware that if the team was to be successful, they would need to simulate, as much as possible, acoustic coding of speech. So he decided to use the six months of sabbatical to fill this gap in his knowledge.

There were two major possible destinations for study that Graeme considered. The first was the Imperial College of London, where he could work with Bruce Sayers, the head of the department of electrical

115

engineering and a pioneer in the field of engineering and medicine. The second was the University of Keele, where Donald MacKay, Bill Ainsworth, Pat Wilson and Ted Evans were located. Graeme was impressed with the work of Donald MacKay, who was head of the Department of Communication and Neuroscience at Keele and whose work he had read. He had also met MacKay in Melbourne where he came to talk about Christian faith and science, and Graeme had been greatly struck by what he had to say. MacKay's openness about how he related his faith and his science appealed to Graeme as they were issues that he also wrestled with. Yet London, when the academic facilities and reputation were taken into account, seemed to Graeme the better option.

In early 1975 Graeme was invited to give a presentation at the British Ear, Nose and Throat Conference in London. This had allowed him the opportunity to visit the facilities at the Imperial College of London. He had also been able to make a quick trip to visit Professor MacKay's laboratories at the University of Keele. Interestingly, the lecture Graeme was invited to give was scheduled alongside nine other options. Only five people signed up for his presentation on his work on the bionic ear. Graeme wondered why he had bothered to come halfway around the world to speak to five people. Then he saw that one of those five was Professor Howard House, a well-known ear surgeon from Los Angeles whose brother William was one of the world's other leading researchers on cochlear implants and who was currently working on a single-electrode device. The connection proved valuable for future contact with the Houses.

Despite his interest in Professor MacKay and his colleagues at Keele, Graeme initially favoured London. While there for the conference he had made arrangements for the family to stay in the Sevenoaks area. But just as he was finalising these arrangements the IRA blew up the carriage of a train travelling between Sevenoaks and central London. Graeme rethought his plans, deciding that the quiet village of Keele, of little interest to the IRA, would be a much safer option. So his sabbatical would be spent at Keele after all. In the end, Graeme was convinced that the best decision had been made both professionally and personally.

In Keele, Graeme was also able to work with Bill Ainsworth in speech science, an area that Graeme knew little about at the time. Graeme later recalled that 'this was a very fruitful time as I learned about synthetic speech and carried out many tests during the three months we were there'. Particularly, Graeme worked on ways to optimise the formants for a Holmes parallel synthesiser, for the purpose of determining the best way to represent consonants. Graeme soon found that some consonants were easier to represent than others, and that in the cases of consonants like 'v' and 'f' there were a few different clues that needed to be picked up. The study Graeme carried out proved invaluable for developing a speech processing strategy when he returned to Melbourne. Graeme also discovered that Donald MacKay's first PhD student, Bruce Millar, was working in Australia, and Graeme was able to build links with him and his work upon returning to Melbourne.

While on sabbatical, Graeme managed to make an important visit to the Speech Research Laboratory in Stockholm where he met with Gunnar Fant and Arne Risberg. While studying in Keele he had discovered their work on vowels that showed that amplitude variation was not very important in vowel recognition. This became significant for Graeme's team later when the hard work began of helping implant recipients to process speech.

Graeme was not only able to learn much from MacKay as a neuroscientist, but he also was able to have long conversations with him about faith. MacKay's strong evangelical views had a big impact on Graeme and Margaret. Graeme recalls that as a scientist and a

Christian, he was quite troubled at the time by the philosophy of determinism, which held that the human brain was nothing but a machine, or as Francis Crick, co-discoverer of the double helix structure of DNA famously put it, 'nothing but a pack of neurons' with the implication that there was no free will. As Graeme later stated the problem: 'If our brains are nothing more than machines and all our thoughts, beliefs and ideas are nothing more than electrical currents determined by other electrical currents, it follows that we have no free will to make any choices.'[49] But this was a view Graeme could not accept. MacKay challenged Graeme to consider that if all our thoughts are predetermined, then we can have no assurance that they are valid. Graeme found this an effective response to his concerns.[50]

Largely due to MacKay's theological influence during their sabbatical in England, the Clarks decided upon their return to Australia, after years of attending Methodist/Uniting congregations, to join the Presbyterian Church in Eltham. They remained members there until 1994, when they followed their daughters to the local Assemblies of God congregation, where they have remained since.

On the family side, during the sabbatical in England, Graeme and Margaret had four young daughters to keep busy. If they were to see the sights of England and if Margaret was to have a way of getting the children around, they would need to buy a vehicle. Graeme and Margaret decided to buy their first new car. They settled on a Peugeot Familiale, which they paid for in instalments, then shipped back to Australia once they were able to save up the money to pay the import duty. As the Clarks were not keen to spend money too often on new cars, they kept the Peugeot as their main family vehicle for the next seventeen years. It became something of an enduring souvenir of their time in England—their children thought they would never see the end of it.

Upon their return to Australia, after all the study and travel, and enduring an English winter, the first thing the Clarks did was to take a belated summer holiday—in Kiama, of course. For Graeme it was a time of refreshment with some enjoyable swims. Little could he have suspected that his next holiday to Kiama would mark one of the decisive turning points in his research.

CHAPTER 19

A day at the beach

One of the most fascinating phenomena in modern science is the role played by serendipity. The number of scientific breakthroughs made outside the laboratory or under unexpected circumstances is significant. While a thorough knowledge of the field and a grasp of the problem at hand are required, in many instances it is the ability to allow other aspects of our lives and our humanity into the picture that opens up new and unexpected ways of approaching what previously seemed an insoluble problem.

One wonders how science might have developed differently, for instance, if 22-year-old Isaac Newton had not been sitting under an apple tree, thinking about his studies, when he was startled by an apple that nearly hit him as it fell to the ground; or if Luigi Galvani had not had a dissected frog lying nearby as he experimented with electricity in 1791; or if a young apprentice book maker, Michael Faraday, who was too poor to go to university, had not stumbled upon the verse from Romans that read 'God's invisible qualities—have been clearly seen', after puzzling over an article on electricity from the volume of the *Encyclopaedia Britannica* he was binding earlier that day . . . or if Graeme Clark had not taken a break, while watching his daughters play in the sand at Minnamurra Beach, to fiddle with a turban shell.

By 1975 Graeme's research was well progressed. Work on a reliable, implantable stimulator was coming along well, the telethons were bringing in much-needed funding, and it seemed only a matter of time before the first surgery for a cochlear implant could be undertaken. But Graeme and his team had become stumped by an unexpected problem. Their device required passing a bundle of electrodes through the spiral coil of the inner ear to the very edge of the brain. On every simulated test they conducted, they found the wires simply would not pass. They were either too thick to bend, or if too thin, simply folded. In trying to force them through, they found some early versions of the electrode bundles sliced through the ear like it was butter. This was particularly a problem when they tried to take them back out of the inner ear. They knew the gold box was a good product. They knew the multi-electrode, multi-channel approach was the most effective. But they needed to find a way to work the bundle of wires safely through the ear to the auditory nerves if it was to be of any use.

On the surface, it seemed like a pretty ordinary problem, compared with the many obstacles that had already been confronted and over-come. To begin with, Graeme made various models of the human inner ear, including acrylic models, and tried passing the wires from below up into the tightening spiral. But they would not go any great distance. Graeme then attempted to insert the electrodes back-to-front by drilling a hole in the apex of the inner ear and passing the bundle downward through the spiral. But he and surgical colleague Brian Pyman determined that the process would cause too much damage to important structures of the inner ear.

Graeme and his team worked on the problem through 1975, experimenting with various options, with no results. Surely with their team of engineers, surgeons and ear specialists they could come up with a solution. The following year passed as well, without a solution. At one stage Graeme had thought 1976 would be a realistic target year for the first implant surgery. Now he was at the end of the year and his team had still not found an effective and safe way of winding the bundle of electrodes down through the inner ear.

Preoccupied with this apparently insurmountable obstacle, Graeme decided to take a break and go on his regular family holiday to Kiama. So January 1977 saw Graeme far removed from his laboratory in Melbourne, sitting on the beach watching his daughters playing in the sand and running among the waves. He began fiddling with a common turban shell, which he chanced to find in the sand, noting how much its structure resembled that of the human inner ear. Then he plucked a blade from a clump of grass growing in the dunes and began to insert it, pointy end first, into the shell. He couldn't believe what was happening. The blade inserted itself smoothly all the way around the spiral and into the shell. He repeated the experiment with other blades of grass and found that it only worked when the thin end was inserted first. Could it be that simple, he wondered?

He tried patiently to wait for the rest of the holiday to pass, but in the end, he couldn't contain his excitement. He decided to pack up the family and head back to Melbourne a couple of days earlier than planned. He was eager to get back to his lab and run some tests. Was it possible that an electrode bundle that was weaker and more flexible at one end than the other would simply follow the course of the inner ear, much like the blade of grass in the turban shell? He did not have to wait long for results. Graeme discovered in his initial tests that tubes of wires with graded stiffness (that is to say, with increasing stiffness towards the rear of the tube) went further into the inner ear without causing damage than anything his team had tried in the previous two years. Thanks to a summer holiday, a convenient turban shell, and a nearby tuft of grass, one of the most difficult engineering problems the team had encountered had been solved. But Graeme and his Australian team were not the only ones beginning to make significant progress in research into a cochlear implant.

shell and a nearly full of gear, one of the most difficult engineering problems the team had encountered had been solved. But Graeme and his Australian team were only the very first, only beginning to make significant progress in turning into a cochlear implant.

CHAPTER 20

The race to code speech

While holiday visits to the beach at Kiama were proving surprisingly productive for Graeme's research, convincing the Australian scientific community that an effective cochlear implant was not only possible, but that it could be achieved in Australia, was another story. There remained no shortage of gainsayers suggesting a workable cochlear implant was not achievable. Nevertheless, by the early 1970s a number of centres around the world, most notably in Los Angeles, Paris, Vienna and Melbourne, believed it was. They were locked in a race to see who would get there first. It had even become widely rumoured that a Nobel Prize would await the team that was able to accomplish the feat. Of these centres, Melbourne stood out initially only for being the least known and least funded.

By 1961 the centre of research into electrical stimulation of the auditory nerves had shifted from France to the United States, to the team led by William House and John and James Doyle in Los Angeles. This team, working with engineer Jack Urban, developed a single-channel implant that was eventually manufactured by the

3M Company and approved for implantation in adults by the US Food and Drug Administration in 1984 (prior to the USDA approval of the Australian cochlear implant). It was eventually implanted in just over a thousand patients.

In the mid-1970s, Professor Claude-Henri Chouard of Paris was experimenting with a device similar to the House model but which used twelve channels and avoided the problem of channel interaction that Graeme's team in Melbourne were then experiencing.[51]

In Vienna, surgeon Kurt Burian and engineer Erwin Hochmair of the Technical University, along with his PhD student and wife Ingeborg Hochmair, developed a device contained within a hermetically sealed glass package. In 1977 Burian implanted the device, containing a multi-electrode cochlear implant, in a patient. The device failed, however, and the team was not able to test it using a speech processor. Another attempt was made in September 1978 using a multi-channel device. Initial tests showed some success in speech recognition and the team worked with only the best of the four electrodes that produced a result. The team initially worked with the 3M Company until the Hochmairs moved to Innsbruck and founded the MED-EL company in 1990, which still produces cochlear implants today.

It has been suggested that 'the two drivers behind the flurry of activity in the cochlear implant area throughout the 1960s and 1970s were progress in electronic engineering and intensive neurosensory research'.[52] In the view of many, the time was right for a major breakthrough in the electrical stimulation of hearing for the deaf.

This was the emerging competitive environment that Graeme and his team entered from early in 1970. They were well aware of other efforts being made. And those overseas were becoming increasingly aware of the progress of the Australian team. Yet, 'despite an environment of many new discoveries [Graeme's] vision was not accepted by his colleagues and his claims were considered to be outrageous'. Blair Simmons, whose work had first inspired Clark, commented that he 'got a distinct impression . . . that most everyone was either incapable of thinking about the many problems involved or would rather not risk tainting their scientific careers'.[53]

Within such a context, few would have put their money on the Australian team to develop the first successful cochlear implant. Indeed, many did not think it likely that any of the competing teams would achieve success.

So why did Clark succeed where others continued to fall short? What was it that was different about his approach that eventually and inevitably led to success?

One observer at the time, Professor Harry Levitt of the City University of New York and, later, Director of Research, Advanced Hearing Concepts, visited Clark in Australia in 1980. He felt that Clark's approach and research stood out against the other major research groups in America and Europe, which tended to focus on relatively narrow aspects of cochlear implants. Levitt observed that, unlike the other research groups at the time:

Clark had a much broader view and his research group addressed all relevant aspects of the problem, including surgical, medical, physiological, psychological and audiological issues, in addition to the crucial technological advances that were needed. A major difference between Professor Clark's approach and that adopted elsewhere was the use of multi-channel as opposed to single-channel stimulation. Multi-channel stimulation allowed for different frequency regions of the cochlea to be stimulated which Professor Clark recognized as a crucial requirement for transmitting speech and other broadband signals.[54]

Graeme's determination to do good science and base his clinical work on this alone, and to do so rigorously, along with his early research-based commitment to pursue the much more difficult multi-channel approach, made all the difference in the end. While the race to produce the first functioning bionic ear seemed at times close, among those who believed it was even possible, the reality was that only Clark and his team were on the right path.

CHAPTER 21

1 August 1978:
The birth of bionics

In the 1970s everyone knew what bionics was. *The Six Million Dollar Man* filled our television screens once a week beginning in 1973. The show was followed a few years later by *The Bionic Woman*. People with bionic implants, we learned through such programs, would have superhuman powers of hearing, of sight, of speed and of strength. Bionics was the ultimate dream of a scientific utopia in which damaged humans could not only be repaired via the use of cybernetic implants, but could be improved upon. As the opening of the popular television series used to say: 'We can rebuild him. We have the technology. We can make him better than he was. Better, stronger, faster.' For the actual pioneers in bionics, however, the aim was not to build a superhuman, but simply to achieve some workable function to replace that which was damaged or that which a person was born without. Superhuman powers were strictly for the realm of science fiction.

Yet until one August day in Melbourne in 1978, bionics of any sort was just that: science fiction. Researchers dreamed of implants for vision, for hearing and even for human limbs that connected electronic implants or prosthetics to human nerves, but none had yet been achieved. A few implants had been attempted to stimulate the auditory nerves, but none of them had yet allowed the patient to actually successfully understand speech—that is until 1 August 1978, a watershed date in medical history—the date that Rod Saunders received what would become the first successful bionic ear implant. Human nerves, for the first time, were integrated effectively with electronics. It was a long way from either the utopian dream of the bionic man, or the science-fiction nightmare of the Borg, but human beings had crossed a frontier. The work being done today on very early versions of bionic eyes and bionic legs continues to slowly but steadily build upon this revolution.

Few at the time were fully aware of the implications and significance of what was being attempted. Graeme Clark, however, was very much aware. He had, after all, 'gambled his entire career on this one outcome'. He knew full well that he was attempting something that had not previously been successfully done, and that many still believed impossible. He knew that in this one venture lay the only real hope to restore hearing for the profoundly deaf. After years of preparation, the weight of the 'moment of truth' bore heavily upon the usually unflappable professor. Graeme had done all the preparations he could do, had assembled the best team he could, had researched thoroughly every aspect of the technology and the surgery.

There was nothing left to do now but prepare himself as best he could. He chose not to spend the lead-up to the surgery with more long hours in the laboratory. Those had already been put in. Instead, he and Margaret went away for a few days of prayer. He also did something else he had never previously done. He sought the prayers of his Presbyterian congregation in Eltham for him, his team and his patient. A week of intercession for divine grace, a congregation praying for him and his patient, and a time of quiet retreat for steadying the nerves, Graeme felt, were the most important things that could be done at that point.

After the surgery on Rod Saunders there was much media interest in the results. The public had become aware of the bionic ear project through the telethons and were keen to know whether the implant had been successful. Graeme's team was not the first to perform such an operation. Devices had been surgically implanted previously in France and in the United States. But they had produced minimal results. It was one thing to surgically implant a package of electronics, such as a bionic ear, into a patient. It was an entirely different matter for it to work. When, after a period of several months of waiting and testing, it became clear that Rod was able to recognise speech via his bionic ear, the announcement was made. A research team in Melbourne, Australia, had developed and implanted the first working bionic ear.

It was the first successful interface between electronics and the human nervous system. The age of bionics was born. But while many celebrated and wondered at this milestone in biomedical history, Graeme and his team pressed on. They knew there was still much more to be done.

CHAPTER 22

More surgeries and the first failures

For Graeme Clark, 1979 was a year of the unexpected. The first surprise was a pleasant one. Margaret informed him that their 'completed' family of four daughters was to be expanded. She was expecting their fifth child in November. Margaret had recently completed a Graduate Diploma in Education so she could return to teaching. Graeme, fresh off the success of his first implant surgery, had much more work to do. And their girls were now all well into their school years, the oldest two already teenagers. This had not been part of the plan.

'It was a surprise,' Graeme admits with a smile. Then Margaret adds quickly, with an even larger smile, 'Yes, but a very pleasant one.' Their son Jonathan was born on 10 November 1979, more than a year after the landmark surgery on Rod Saunders, and just under a decade after the birth of the Clarks' youngest daughter, Merran. Jonathan was to be surrounded by a queue of babysitters and more female attention than he may have liked. But all agreed he was a very welcome addition to the Clark family.

The other surprises for Graeme that year were less pleasant. After the initial success with Rod, the team—and the media—had high expectations. But the next two implants did not go as smoothly. This meant not only much frustration and delays in progress, but much stress for the patients. It was a sign that there was still a great deal of work to be done before the devices could be commercially produced and made available on a broad scale. For Graeme and his team, it was very much a sense of two steps forward, one step backward. But they pressed on, buoyed by the knowledge gained from their experience with Rod, and with their second patient George, that the implant did work.

Some argued that with the success of the first and second implants, it would be best for Graeme and his team to operate on as many patients as possible to gather as much data as they could. Also, Paul Trainor from Nucleus (formerly Telectronics) wanted at least three successful patients before he felt he could take the risk of moving the product towards commercial development. Graeme understood this need, but his own approach was one of cautious progress. He recalls, 'There was an attitude in surgery that your success depended upon the number of cases that you operated on. I did not agree with this policy. I felt you could learn more from careful study on a small group of patients and therefore minimise the risk to others.' Graeme did not want to accumulate a large number of minimally successful results. Instead, he wanted better results and felt this could be done more ethically and successfully with a small number of patients. Graeme was just as concerned for the wellbeing of his patients as he was with the success of the bionic ear project. 'My aim,' Graeme recalls, 'was to put patient welfare first and not treat them as guinea pigs to find out basic information.' So it was that Graeme chose to continue to proceed slowly.

George Watson, who had been disappointed not to have been selected as the first bionic ear recipient, was the next patient Graeme chose for the surgery. Graeme was committed to continuing slowly, with one patient at a time, making sure they got it right. Like Rod, George had lost his hearing as an adult, but he had now been profoundly deaf for thirteen years, much longer than Rod. Although disappointed not to have had the surgery in 1978, George was still very keen. The team was interested to learn whether the prolonged length of time George had been deaf would make it more difficult for him to learn to process speech using the cochlear implant. For these reasons he was the most logical candidate for the next surgery.

While George was committed to the procedure, he still had a lot of questions. His main concern was that he didn't want to finish up as a 'vegetable'. As with Rod, Graeme had developed a genuine fondness for George and wanted to answer his questions as best he could. But, as he explained to George in one meeting, 'This is an entirely new field, not much research has been done in the area before. Not everybody is suitable for this early research. We want people who will be patient and don't mind coming in for tests and retraining.' What little was known for certain had come largely from the team's experience with Rod Saunders. What Graeme could and did tell George, however, was this: 'We don't have to repeat all the same things in such detail with you as we did with Rod . . . We still cannot guarantee speech although we are doing our best to achieve it.'[55]

George Watson's operation took place on 13 July 1979. The procedure went smoothly and more quickly due to the team's experience with Rod. Graeme recalls, 'George was a wonderful patient, and I well remember the day after the operation he came down in the lift and visited me in the department.'

In fact, George recovered so quickly that Graeme and his team decided to operate on their next patient, Joan Keetley, two weeks later. Joan had lost her hearing through meningitis thirty-five years earlier. How she would respond to the auditory stimulation of the cochlear implant after the auditory nerves had gone so long without any signals would be very significant. More importantly, the team now had two patients they could work with more or less in tandem. Joan had had great optimism about the surgery, and had written to Graeme after Rod's surgery with the words: 'For you, the winter has been long and hard, but when the summer comes it will be all the more glorious.'[56]

But Graeme encountered an unexpected problem when operating on Joan. The X-rays had not revealed that her inner ear had been completely shut by a plug of bone. Despite the team's efforts to drill along the lower canal, the plug did not clear. Graeme then noticed the top of the tube was still open. This was the only remaining site where an implant could possibly be inserted. If he continued on, he would risk damage that would eliminate the chance for a future, improved implant that could fit into this site. If he didn't continue, there might not be another opportunity. Graeme found the decision agonising but had little time to decide. He chose to abort the operation and preserve the remaining channel for an improved device that might one day soon be available. It was a decision he still regrets.

Joan was bitterly disappointed. The whole team, as well as George Watson who was still recovering at the Eye and Ear, were saddened for Joan and for the program. The operation Graeme thought he could perform in the future once he learned how current flowed through solid bone proved not to be possible due to later illness suffered by Joan. Because he had not proceeded with the surgery at the time, Joan lost her chance to receive a bionic ear. For someone whose main motivation had always been to help the deaf to hear, it was a bitter blow. It was also Graeme's first significant failure since the program had begun.

Meanwhile the news, initially, was much better for George Watson. He was making quick progress. After just a few sessions the team brought in the morning paper and read it to him. He was able to hear and understand speech. This meant that the processing strategy they had developed and which had worked successfully for Rod Saunders was not unique to him. It could work for anyone.

But the team still needed a third patient to satisfy Phase 1 funding demands and demonstrate the viability of the implants for a range of patients. Another female patient was referred and another surgery scheduled. The initial results were again good and she could hear some sounds. But then something began to go wrong.

The patient began to experience strange and unpredictable sensations. The team tested everything to find why the implant was failing. In the end they came to the conclusion that the sealed gold box that was the heart of the bionic ear had developed a leak. The device had failed.

It was found that soldering the two halves of the implant package together had not worked. The team would need to find a better way of sealing the gold box. Graeme appeared to have had two successes in Rod and George, and two failures, with two very disappointed patients and their families. While the results shown by Rod and George were sufficient indication that the cochlear implant did work, a 50 per cent failure rate was simply not acceptable.

Graeme, with Margaret and the children, went to Kiama for their annual summer holidays. He needed time to think about what had gone wrong. When he returned he was in for more unpleasant news. George had reported hearing odd bangs and hissing sounds in his ear. At first they occurred only occasionally. But then they increased. By April, the device had failed completely. While the failure of the seal again was found to be at the heart of the problem, this was compounded by the fact that George had a tendency to fall asleep before taking his receiver off. Turning back and forth in the night had caused damage to the receiver wires.

Significantly, during the nine months that George's implant had functioned, a great deal of essential information was gained that played a vital role in the further development of the device and the understanding of how speech is processed. As George had been deaf for much longer than Rod had been, his ability to process speech with the implant showed that memory for speech sounds could remain in the brain even after prolonged deafness. So in a sense, George's initial implant, while ultimately failing, proved to be an important success in terms of research and development.

At the time, however, the failure of George's implant was not only disheartening for both George and Graeme, it put Graeme and his project in a very difficult position. Graeme had done, or attempted, four operations. He had successfully implanted three devices. But he now had only one patient with a functioning cochlear implant: Rod Saunders. The sceptics were again beginning to circle. One researcher even claimed that Graeme must have fabricated the results in the case of Rod Saunders. It was claimed that Rod was only lip-reading. Others were saying that the multi-electrode device had not been able to produce significantly better results than the single electrode devices developed by the other teams around the world, which had proved useful largely only as an aid to lip-reading.

The situation was especially critical, as a major government grant to assist with the commercial development of the project was on the line, and a major press conference, featuring Rod and George, had been scheduled. If the government funding committee found out that George's device was no longer working, the funding could easily be lost. Both Rod and George appeared and were presented to the press, but Rod did most of the talking. Graeme remembers how relieved he felt that the press did not ask George any leading questions. The fact that George, who had been deaf for much longer than Rod, had learned to lip-read enabled him to bluff his way through the

136

questioning, leaving the press with the impression that his device was still working—without either he or Graeme actually claiming that it was. This was a technicality Graeme was more than happy to live with at the time. The government grant was announced shortly afterwards.

But a clear problem existed and needed to be solved. There was some pressure to use a package with glass seals, as developed by one of the competing teams in Vienna. Graeme was reluctant to do this as he felt it was important to make this an all-Australian project, and not import the technology. Yet he was not willing to let the project fail on account of his national pride. In the end he decided for other reasons not to go with the glass seals. This turned out to be fortuitous as it was soon discovered that they, too, leaked.

Graeme and his team—together with the newly formed Cochlear Limited—were eventually able to solve the problem of the leaking seals through the use of a ceramic to metal seal. By 1982 they had six implant patients at the Eye and Ear. They were also finally in a position to commence a worldwide clinical trial. In 1984 the team began implanting people who spoke languages other than English. It was not certain that the speech coding would work as well for languages other than English, particularly those that were markedly different. In April 1984 a Mandarin speaker from Malaysia, Beng Kim Lee, was operated on by Clark and his team. A Chinese-speaking doctor constructed the language tests, with results that surpassed even those of the existing English-speaking patients. The device clearly worked for all language types. One US researcher, Professor Bob White of Stanford University, was so impressed by the results from Mr Lee and the ability of the equipment to process Mandarin speech sounds that he quipped, 'All deaf people should learn Mandarin!' [57]

CHAPTER 23

The faith of a scientist

In the course of his career Graeme had noticed that scientists who had a strong religious faith, and were open about this faith, were not very common. He had been impressed since his student years with Charles Birch and Donald MacKay. More recently, he had also read and been inspired by the writings of the physicist Sir John Polkinghorne, who at the height of his career had become an Anglican priest. As Graeme's own profile grew, he could not escape the feeling that he owed it to all those Christians who felt somehow fearful of or intimidated by science to speak clearly about his own faith. He had also become concerned that many Christians he knew through church and elsewhere seemed to feel that the theory of evolution excluded a faith in God as creator.

So with Birch, MacKay and Polkinghorne as examples, and his first successful implant surgery now behind him, Graeme decided it was time to make a contribution to this contentious area of the relationship between faith and science. This was something of a new field for Graeme, but the fear of entering into new fields had never stopped him before. Graeme decided to produce a booklet with four chapters. First, he felt a history of science, especially as it related to Christian faith, was needed in order to show the many historical links between people of faith and people of science. Next, Graeme wrote about the nature of science and scientists, seeking to correct a number of myths and misconceptions that some Christians had. Then he felt he needed to include a chapter on evolution and creation, which was such a vexing topic for so many. Finally, he concluded with a chapter on neuroscience and faith. The booklet, *Science and God: Reconciling science with the Christian faith*, appeared in 1979.

After all the controversies and opposition he had experienced within the medical and scientific communities in his work to develop a bionic ear, Graeme thought the field of theology would be much less of a minefield. This was a miscalculation. Despite three very useful, insightful and relatively non-controversial chapters, it was the chapter on creation and evolution that unleashed controversy.

What Graeme hoped to achieve was to voice the concerns of those Christians who had suspicions about evolution, so that they would feel their voices were being heard, while leaving the door open enough that these same people might see that evolution was not necessarily incompatible with Christian faith. Instead, the secular press took Graeme to be an anti-evolution creationist, and he was pilloried for this. The anti-evolution creationists, on the other hand, clearly picked up that Graeme, despite giving their concerns much due, fell short of affirming their position. Hence they also rejected his work. For Graeme, it was an unexpected reaction from both sides. He decided to make no further public forays into the area of faith and science. For those seeking to show that the two can work together, this was unfortunate. Many would have liked to hear more from Graeme about neuroscience and faith, or about the way a Christian who is also a scientist looks at nature. But Graeme decided that he had enough conflict and opposition already in his work with the bionic ear, and to leave theology alone.

It was nearly four decades later, when Richard Dawkins, Sam Harris and Daniel Dennett came to Melbourne in 2012 for The Global Atheist Convention, a major gathering of the so-called New Atheists, that Graeme was persuaded to clarify his own views on faith and science. It bothered him that some leading scientists were suggesting that Christian faith and evolutionary theory could not live together. It also bothered him still that many within both the scientific and faith communities thought he was an anti-evolution creationist. So Graeme released a media statement in the context of the Melbourne event that was not critical of Dawkins and his fellow speakers, but simply sought to clarify his own views and demonstrate that a scientist could be both an evolutionist and an evangelical Christian.

Perhaps not surprisingly neither the secular nor the religious press paid it much attention. Both were looking for a head-on attack of Dawkins, or perhaps a rejection of evolution. There was no longer much newsworthy, it seemed, about a Christian and a scientist saying that evolution and Christian faith were compatible. Nevertheless, after the controversy and confusion over his 1979 booklet, Graeme thought that it still merited saying.

His statement, especially in light of the confusion about what he was trying to accomplish in his 1979 publication, is significant not only for his views on evolution and creation, but also for his approach to faith and science. Graeme wrote:

Since my first studies in Anatomy in my medical course at the University of Sydney I have been convinced the theory of evolution as enunciated by Charles Darwin and Alfred Wallace was a beautiful explanation of how life developed on earth. In fact one of my first scientific papers was entitled 'Evolution and Function in the Middle Ear'.[58]

For Graeme, being a Christian and a scientist had little if anything to do with what he thought about evolution. What was most important was the strength and courage his faith gave him when the task at hand seemed impossible. Graeme's faith was not about positions on matters such as evolution and creation, but about the relationship he had with God and how this gave him strength. He wrote:

> For me it has been a roller coaster ride through joys and disappointments, successes and failures. Faith in God, Father, Son and Holy Spirit was integral to my scientific journey. I could not have kept going without the sense that this God of love had given me the opportunity to do something to help deaf people. So I prayed about each step to take and I believe God guided the decisions to be made and provided the resources to help—both the people who joined the team and the finances as it was needed. When there was opposition I tried as best I could to deal with it the way Jesus did, and take the attitude, 'If we fail, we fail,' because God does not guarantee success.[59]

And while many in the community are under the impression that science and personal faith in God are at odds with one another, Graeme saw encouragement in the sciences for his faith. In fact, he felt that recent advances in scientific knowledge actually made faith easier, or at least helped to give it intellectual credibility. In particular, Graeme listed six specific insights or discoveries of science which have strengthened his own faith journey:

1. The big bang theory showed the universe was not eternal but had a beginning.
2. The incredible fine-tuning of the universe for life has shown how improbable it would have been without a guiding principle.
3. The convergence of biological evolution to a limited number

of optimal solutions indicates early guided development. For example, the camera eye seen in humans and the octopus.

4. Quantum physics describes the unpredictable operation of electrons at the subatomic level, while the butterfly effect of chaos theory described by Edward Lorenz reflects the interconnected reality of the universe and suggests, again, a guiding principle behind apparent random activity.

5. Randomness is compatible with our intuitive experience as well as the biblical doctrine of freedom to act, which in turn establishes moral responsibility (so argues Paul Ewart, professor of physics at Oxford).

6. The 'instruction manual' in the human genome mirrors the concept of the Word or Logos of St John's gospel and 'God said'. This is reflected also in the work of Francis Collins, who led the team which mapped the human genome, in his book *The Language of God*.[60]

For Graeme, there was never much interest in engaging in debate about creation and evolution. And he was certainly not interested either in debating or criticising Dawkins or those of similar views. Dawkins had every right to his views, and despite the urging of some, Graeme was not going to criticise them. The best response was simply to state how he saw the world through the eyes of science and faith. Graeme felt it was important to dispel the idea that a Christian could not be a good and successful scientist. He had never felt that his faith prevented him from working with foundational scientific theories, like evolution. Nor had he ever felt that these theories threatened his faith; quite the opposite. The more he saw of the wonder of evolution, the wonder of human hearing and the human brain, the wonder of nature in all its grandeur, the more he sensed the presence of a loving God.

CHAPTER 24

Federal funding
at last

Successfully implanting a bionic ear and showing that it actually worked was a huge achievement. Most would have thought that the initial implant successes meant 'mission accomplished'. But having a few surgical successes meant little if the cochlear implants could not be made commercially viable and available to a wide number of patients. And for Graeme, all the work and creativity done by Australians would seem to have benefited the nation little if the technology was simply developed commercially in Europe or North America. This had happened all too often in the past with Australian innovations and Graeme was determined to see that it did not happen with the bionic ear. But this, of course, meant that his work was far from over. Even in the lead-up to that first successful surgery, Graeme recognised what needed to be done, and knew that it could not be achieved without significant government support.

Graeme's earlier efforts to gain government research funding had had very limited success. He felt, however, that with the publicity achieved and the progress already made, and the first implant surgery on Rod Saunders imminent, another effort to gain government funding should be made. He and his team had made an application for funding already to the minister of productivity in the Fraser government, Ian McPhee AO, but were yet to receive a reply.

Graeme decided to go straight to the top with his request, writing a letter to the prime minister, Malcolm Fraser, on 20 July 1978. He pointed out to Mr Fraser that the European Economic Community had agreed to fund a joint project to have a commercial product available by early 1980 and that the North Americans were not far behind. He noted that the University of Melbourne was ahead of the Europeans and Americans in terms of research at the moment, but this edge and the potential to capitalise on their research commercially would be lost if they did not get developmental funding from the government. Graeme concluded his letter with a simple request. 'I would be pleased,' he wrote, 'if the Government could develop the project which I believe to be in the national interest for a number of sound reasons. Yours sincerely, Graeme M Clark, Professor of Otolaryngology.' It was a long shot, but Graeme had nothing to lose.

To his surprise, he received a very favourable reply from the prime minister dated 28 July 1978, just days before the first implant operation was scheduled to occur. Mr Fraser responded:

Dear Professor Clark

Thank you for your letter of 20 July concerning the artificial hearing device developed by the University of Melbourne for surgical implantation into patients who are profoundly deaf.

Your letter highlights the need to capitalise on Australia's current lead in this field, particularly in the light of the planned developments in Europe and North America. In this respect, you will notice that the 1978/79 budget provides for enhanced Government

144

support for industrial research and development including the provision of support for the undertaking of 'public interest' research projects.

I am aware that the Minister for Productivity is giving careful consideration to providing appropriate assistance for the commercial development of this Australian innovation as a public interest project and I understand that a decision on your application is anticipated in the near future.

Finally, I would like to express my appreciation at your own research contribution to this potentially important development and also for your continuing efforts towards transferring the results of this research to Australian industry.

Yours sincerely,

Malcolm Fraser [61]

The process had been jump-started, and the research centre was about to receive the funding boost needed to take the bionic ear project to the next level.

On 31 January 1979, Minister for Productivity Ian McPhee announced a one-million dollar grant to extend over a period of two years to assist with the commercial development of the cochlear implant. As part of this process, firms were invited to express tenders of interest to be involved in the commercial development of the implant. While some initial interest was shown by overseas market giant 3M, a little known Australian company called Nucleus (formerly known as Telectronics), which made pacemakers and other medical devices and was led by Paul Trainor, was eventually announced as the successful tenderer. Nucleus, which later developed a subsidiary named Cochlear Limited, had the major advantage that it already had a history of manufacturing and selling implantable devices. Nucleus, through Cochlear Limited, was to become one of the most successful biotechnological companies in Australia, and on the world scene. But that is a story for another chapter.

Amazingly, professional opposition was still a serious problem to contend with. In July 1979 Graeme was quite shocked to get a letter from the government funding body asking for a justification of the viability of the program. As it turned out, an Australian professor of physics had complained to the government that the funding for commercial development of the bionic ear was a waste, claiming that there was a group at Stanford University in America that was doing the same thing, and was much further progressed than the Australian effort. This complaint was lodged despite the fact that it was Graeme Clark and his team in Melbourne who had developed the multi-channel cochlear implant, and were so far the only team to successfully surgically implant the device. Graeme, who was well aware of the work of the Stanford group, had to explain to the government why the Australian concept was actually commercially more viable and worth funding. He summarised his arguments as follows:

- The Stanford team used a bayonet-shaped electrode into the inner ear near where it entered the brain, which was potentially more damaging and more risky than the Australian design.
- The Stanford team used four electrodes instead of the ten used by the Australian team, which gave them much less scope for successful speech processing.
- The link between the external component and their version of the gold box was ultrasonic, which Graeme's team, through careful research, had already shown was less reliable than the radio frequencies they used.
- The initial clinical results from speech processing from the cochlear implant of the Australian team were clearly superior to those produced so far by the Stanford team.[62]

In the end, Graeme was able to point out that the US team was playing catch-up to the Australians with an inferior product and were much further behind in both testing and results. They were not likely to deliver a product of as high a standard in the end. His argument was enough. The funding was confirmed and Graeme and his team were able to continue their work, but left to wonder where the next objection would come from.

As late as 1980 it seemed to Graeme that 3M was to be the major player in the market and that the Australians would need to somehow work with them. But the situation changed quickly when Graeme learned that 3M was not interested in a multi-channel device. They had been relying heavily on the research and advice of Dr William House in the United States, who had a very good reputation and a broad network of contacts in the ENT community. House, of course, had been focusing his work on a single-channel implant, and 3M appears to have felt this was the least expensive and easiest way to enter the market. Graeme and his team were still not well known in the United States. Apart from the team's own research into single-versus multi-channel implants, there was little evidence that the single-channel devices being championed in the United States would be particularly effective.

With 3M going in a very different direction to Graeme and his team, Graeme realised he was going to need to continue to rely heavily on government support for the commercialisation of the project in addition to finding a manufacturing partner. Graeme's team would not be working in partnership with 3M, as they had once thought, but would be going up against them commercially. Graeme felt like David going up against Goliath. Once again, Graeme recognised the need to pray and to trust God. In the end, he concluded that even in the commercial world, which was largely foreign to him, if he and his team did the best they could and sought to produce a product that

147

would ultimately be of most benefit to deaf people, then this was the best way to go.

Graeme looked for help anywhere he could find it. In 1976 he made a trip to Adelaide to talk to the people at the Weapons Research Establishment (now Defence Science and Technology Organisation) in the hope that there may be some overlap in technology. While there, he got a call informing him that an additional grant might be available for the project, but he would have to catch the next flight back to Melbourne to meet with the new minister for productivity, Senator Kevin Newman, who would be in the city briefly on his way back to Canberra. As luck would have it, Graeme already knew Kevin. They had served together as prefects at The Scots College in Sydney. Graeme hurried home and made his case. The old scholars connection through The Scots College proved unnecessary. Newman was already sold on the merits of the project and Graeme's team soon received word that they had the additional grant.

ceramic solution to the problem was found. This was vital not only for the future of commercial production but for the university team's continued research as well. At this stage they still had only one patient, Rod Saunders, with a working device.

The year 1981 was spent largely on developing the kind of clinical trials that the Food and Drug Administration (FDA) in America would find acceptable. If the bionic ear was going to be commercially viable, then the crucial US market would have to be cracked. Also, the team would have to develop training manuals for surgeons who would be implanting the devices. The implant surgery, though now successfully performed several times, was still very complex. A comprehensive knowledge of the operation, as well as the technology of the devices themselves, would be necessary for a broad uptake of the cochlear implants. Many of those early manuals Graeme developed were eventually included in his definitive 800-page textbook, *Cochlear Implants: Fundamentals and applications*, which covered the history, surgical procedures, technology, patient care and speech training associated with the cochlear implants. Published in 2003, it remains the standard text in the field.[64]

In the 1980s, however, the needs were more specific and limited. The cochlear implants would need to be trialled not only in centres in Australia, but also in America, if FDA approval was to be gained. A major problem that Graeme and his team faced, however, was that at this time many ear surgeons were trialling the House single-channel device in the United States. Many 'amateurish' products were also being produced, especially in France, which had once held the lead in this field. None of these products had FDA or any other body's approval, but were all technically a part of one clinical trial or another.

Telectronics had much riding on solving the problem of the leaking seal, and they could not take a product to market without strong evidence that the device worked, and worked reliably. By September

1982 Telectronics and Clark believed they had their product. Graeme and his team, which included Dr Brian Pyman and Dr Robert Webb, performed the surgery on Graham Carrick. He became the first recipient of the commercial prototype bionic ear, and only the fourth recipient of a bionic ear from Graeme's team. While the surgery on Rod Saunders had been the landmark development for Clark's University of Melbourne team, the surgery on Graham Carrick took on similar significance for the team at Telectronics. Graeme Clark was also very much aware that the commercial version of the product needed to work if they were to convince centres outside Australia to conduct clinical trials.

The surgery was performed successfully, and a couple of weeks later the technical team was on hand to turn on the processor. As the project was now being funded by the federal government, the room contained not only Graeme Clark and the technical team from Telectronics, but also a number of political representatives and members of the press. If the device didn't work, there would be no covering up the failure. With great expectation the switch was turned on. Nothing happened. In fact, for fifteen full minutes nothing happened. Carrick did not hear a single sound. Then, as Carrick explains, 'It hit me, I heard a "ding dong" and I said to myself "bloody hell!"' As he described it later, 'To get this sound was fascinating and mind boggling. Tears ran down my face.'[65] And so the commercial version of the bionic ear was born.

But Clark still had to convince surgeons overseas to give the Australian device a go. He began working through the list of significant contacts he had made at ENT conferences where he had presented papers about his work. Graeme passed these contacts on to Mike Hirshorn and Dianne Mecklenburg, who followed them up. Several of these bore fruit. By the end of 1983 surgeries were being conducted in Australia, the United States and Europe using the Australian-made device under clinical trial conditions.

While the trials were progressing, Graeme and his team continued to work hard on improving their product, especially the performance of their speech processor. And Paul Trainor, CEO David Money and their team at Nucleus were working equally hard to improve the manufacture of the implants. The relationship with Telectronics turned out to be fortuitous. Telectronics—because of their experience producing hermetically sealed pacemakers, and with the team Paul Trainor was able to assemble—was probably the only company in Australia at that time in a position to successfully take the product into commercial production and market it internationally.

Graeme, for his part, was keen to see a commercial venture established to take the cochlear implant into production. While he chose to remain as a professor and researcher at the University of Melbourne, supporting the work in this way, he was happy when Paul Trainor approached him about hiring key members from his team to come over to what was soon to become Cochlear Limited in order to ensure continuity of the project. Chief among those early team members who joined Nucleus was engineer Jim Patrick, who went on to become a vice president and the chief scientist of Cochlear Limited.

In the end, the Australian product proved superior to every other device being trialled. In 1985 it became the first multi-channel cochlear implant device to receive FDA approval for implantation in adults. The continued research during the trials and the work with Paul Trainor and his company meant the Australians were now in a position to dominate the market in cochlear implants—something few would have imagined even as recently as 1982.

When the bionic ear—developed by Graeme Clark and his team and produced by the company that would eventually become Cochlear Limited—was officially approved by the FDA in 1985, it had 90 per cent of the US market and 70 per cent of the European market. By 2014 Australian-made cochlear devices had been implanted in more than 250,000 recipients and Cochlear Limited remains today the leading producer of bionic ear implants around the world, with approximately 70 per cent of the international market. This overwhelming success meant the commercial production of the bionic ear was the first major advance in helping the deaf since the development of sign language in the Paris Deaf School two hundred years earlier.

But all this may never have been achieved without the vision and persistence of one man in the face of all obstacles. The commercial success of the cochlear implant had much to do with not only Paul Trainor and his innovative team at Cochlear Limited, but also with the unique attitude and approach of Graeme Clark, who was not willing to allow another Australian innovation to be produced overseas if it could be avoided. As Professor Ed Byrne, head of the Medical School of University College London, observed: 'Without his dedication it is doubtful if a commercially viable product would have made it to the market.'[66]

As Bondarew and Seligman note in the introduction to *The Cochlear Story*, Graeme Clark, unlike many researchers, 'lobbied government and interest groups for critical funding while managing the disdain of colleagues ... to achieve the dream'.[67] But Graeme recognised his limitations. He was more concerned in making the cochlear implant available on a broad commercial scale, and by an Australian company if at all possible, than in clinging to control of his invention.

He also understood the need to hand over the reins to someone who had experience in the commercialisation process. 'Many scientific entrepreneurs feel that because they have driven the research ... they are qualified to lead the commercialisation process. It is their baby, their invention and it is hard to let it go. Graeme Clark was not one of those.'[68]

CHAPTER 26

Implants for children

While the process of clinical trials for adults was going well, and an emerging market was beginning to develop for the Australian-made cochlear implant, Graeme knew that the future of the device would rest upon its ability to help deaf children. Because of the lack of brain plasticity in adults, those born deaf were able to receive only limited benefit from an implant once they had reached adulthood. Graeme's research indicated that there was in Australia alone a significant number of hearing adults who had become deaf through injury or disease who could benefit from the devices. Yet the real need, Graeme had believed from the beginning, was to be able to help children born deaf. But while all indications pointed to the devices likely being effective for deaf children, no one yet knew this with certainty. Performing the implant operation on children, especially young children, brought with it a number of difficulties and would have to be approached very cautiously.

Getting volunteers among adults to trial the new implants, despite the opposition of many ear doctors, was relatively straightforward compared with the possibility of operating on children. The first adult recipients had all started life with at least partial hearing ability. They knew what speech was supposed to sound like and could articulate well to Graeme and his team how they perceived the speech sounds they were experiencing through the implants. They were able to understand the risks and limitations of the surgery and make an informed decision. As a research scientist and surgeon, Graeme was well aware of the complex issues involved in doing pioneering work with children and was unwilling to rush. As Graeme explained, 'A fault in an adult could be explained to them as part of the risk . . . but children are not mature enough to make decisions that will affect their whole life, and a failure could have serious psychological effects.'[69]

But if the dream of opening up the world of sound and speech perception to those born deaf was going to be achieved, the procedure would have to be trialled on young children. Children learn at a much quicker rate than adults, and if the deaf were to learn to hear with a cochlear implant, then they would need to begin this process as children. Given the advantages that had been found in pioneering the implants with adults who had previously had hearing, the decision was made to trial the implants first on children who had previously experienced hearing so that Graeme and his team could gather more accurate information about how the implants worked with children.

By the mid-1980s the implants were becoming increasingly recognised as a safe and successful procedure, so the process of finding child candidates was made somewhat easier. Yet there were difficulties. US implant teams working with their own product had remained committed to single-electrode implants, despite the fact these had been shown to be inferior to the Australian product, and had already implanted them in children as early as 1980. But they were found to have minimal beneficial results for children as far as speech recognition was concerned. Graeme and his team had to overcome the stigma of these failures and convince all involved that their device was quite different from what the Americans were using, their research more thorough, and the chances for success much greater. Once Graeme and his team had convinced the university ethics committee that the surgery was safe and would likely lead to a successful outcome, it only remained to find a suitable candidate for the Australian-made device.

Scott Smith, from the Melbourne suburb of Sunshine, had come down with a severe case of meningitis when he was three years old. He gradually lost his hearing and speech ability through the impact of the disease. The best hearing aids could do little more than produce sensations of vibration for Scott. A once happy and talkative boy had become profoundly deaf and was struggling to cope. Scott's parents, Alan and Betty Smith, enrolled him in a special school for the deaf. But Scott's behaviour continued to be a problem and he eventually refused to wear hearing aids, which helped him little in any event. Desperate, Scott's mother Betty rang a leading audiologist, wondering whether someday anything might be possible to help Scott to hear again. The audiologist, Peter Cichello, had been following the progress of Graeme's team and the bionic ear. He knew they were considering trialling the device with children. He told Betty, and sent her some information about the implants. After some consideration, Betty decided to ring up the Melbourne University Department of Otolaryngology.[70] She was told to bring Scott in for an assessment, but was informed that no implants were being done at that time on children, and that she should not get her hopes up.

The timing, however, turned out to be right. Graeme's team was closer than many had realised to trialling the implants with younger children, and Scott looked to be an ideal candidate. The gold box as well as the external components had all been further miniaturised, making them more suitable for children. After a number of assessments and meetings the team decided Scott was a good candidate for surgery. His parents explained to him that he could get his hearing back.

But there was a hitch. Both Scott and his father were very keen on sport. Scott loved cricket and Australian Rules Football and was captain of his under eleven football team. Graeme remembers that he hated to disappoint Scott, as he himself had been a keen sportsman in his youth. But he had to tell him that 'sports with body contact like cricket and football were risky'. Perhaps, Graeme added, holding out only a little hope, he might be able to play some sports again while wearing a special helmet, but there were no guarantees. It was not an easy decision for Scott, but in the end, his desire to hear again outweighed his love of playing sport. Aware of Scott's passion, Graeme and his team decided to schedule the surgery after the last football game of the season.

After a delay due to an inflammation of the inner ear, the milestone surgery was finally carried out on 20 August 1985 at the Eye and Ear. While the surgery went well, what followed confirmed to Graeme the complexities of working with children. When the device was switched on two weeks after the surgery Scott became very agitated and wanted it taken out. He didn't like it all. It took a lot of gentle coaching from audiologist Dianne Mecklenburg to get Scott to give it a try. The current was turned up very slowly. Scott was disappointed just to hear a lot of crackling. He said later that he thought he would be able to hear people speaking straight away. Graeme realised that much more care needed to be taken in future to communicate very clearly to children what to expect.

It took some time to run the tests to work through faults in the wearable speech processor. All of this was quite normal. Then, of course, the current levels had to be properly set and Scott needed to be trained to hear speech. It took nine months to achieve what Scott had expected to be an immediate result, but in the end, both Scott and Graeme were very pleased with what he was able to understand. He was making even better progress than teenager Peter Searle, who had been the youngest recipient up to that point. It seemed, Graeme reflected, that younger patients have more 'plasticity' in their hearing pathways. The case for implants in children, in Graeme's view, was building. And Scott did play football again with the use of a special helmet, and went on the following year to once again captain his Australian Rules Football team.[71]

Taking on board the lessons they had learned from Peter Searle and Scott Smith, Graeme and his team next operated on six-year-old Bryn Davies in April 1986. Again, Bryn had been born with hearing and, like Scott, had lost his hearing through childhood meningitis when he was three. His surgery was also a success and Bryn, like Scott, slowly learned all over again how to hear.

The Americans, in the view of some, may have moved too hastily to implant children as early as 1980, and the results had been minimal. The Europeans would not carry out their first implant on a young child until 1988, the British not until the following year, and the Japanese would not implant their first child with a bionic ear until 1991. Graeme remembers that 'by 1988 we thought that the controversy surrounding implanting children would have started to abate, but it was still a hot issue'. One problem was that it took time for children to adapt and learn to use the devices, and they experienced frustrations that adults did not. Every time an implanted device failed or did not work as well as expected in a child, it was lifted up as a typical example of the limitations of the bionic ear with children.

Special care had to be taken with children every step of the way. Graeme was always particularly concerned with the psychological impact of undergoing major surgery, and adapting to a whole new world of sound. He and his team did everything they could to minimise any negative impact on children. The team even arranged for a toy car that the younger children could drive to the operating theatre for their surgeries. Even then, Graeme recalls, he and his team had to be 'courageous in order to operate on children at younger and younger ages'.

The results that Graeme's team, and now many others, were achieving with bionic ear implants in children could not be ignored. The floodgates had opened wide to a whole new world of sound for deaf children.

CHAPTER 27

Even children born deaf shall hear

Younger and younger children were being fitted with bionic ear implants. But still, they had all been children who had had hearing at one time. The question Graeme really wanted to know the answer to was whether the multi-electrode, multi-channel cochlear implant he and his team had developed and then improved upon over so many years would be effective for children born deaf. Graeme, as was his nature, was determined to press forward, but only with the utmost caution and preparation. Implanting the device in a young child who was born deaf was going to be a significant learning experience for the team. It would not be the same as working with a child who could remember once being able to hear and recognise words. And if the team, to some extent, would be venturing again into the unknown, so too would the child.

To prepare for operating on children born deaf, Graeme performed implants for two adults, both in their early twenties, who had been born deaf and were taught sign language. But because they had never learned as children to recognise speech, they had developed

161

a fundamental defect in the way their brains responded to sound. Graeme found that neither patient was able to hear sounds in the way that adults who had learned to hear before going deaf had been able to do. There was no ability to hear a different pitch or timbre. The devices didn't even appear to help with lip-reading. The only useful function they provided was to alert the wearers to the presence of sound. It was sadly apparent that for those born deaf, once the brain no longer had the developmental plasticity associated with childhood, the benefits of a bionic ear were limited.

For this reason Graeme next chose to work first with a teenager, fourteen-year-old Colleen Tarrant. While her age meant it would be easier for her to cope with the process, she was also nearly at the age where the brain ceases to be plastic and its ability to adapt would be too severely restricted for the implant to be fully effective. Graeme would in many ways have liked to begin with a younger patient, but he was also keen to see if there was still enough plasticity in the brain of a fourteen-year-old to benefit from an implant. In addition, Graeme found Colleen's case personally pressing. These were, after all, not science experiments he was working with but real human beings with real needs.

Colleen was not only born deaf, but she was also born with severe vision impairment. In a few years' time she would be completely blind, and then would not even have access to sign language as a form of communication. If the team did not operate quickly, they would lose what little window of opportunity was left for her brain to take advantage of its elastic stage of development. So Graeme scheduled surgery for April 1987. The post-operative process of learning to use the bionic ear was slow, but it was soon apparent that it was of immediate assistance with lip-reading, and would also be useful once Colleen could no longer see. She was the first child born deaf to receive a multi-electrode cochlear implant from Graeme's team.

In a sign of the success and progress of the cochlear implant, the second child born deaf to receive the device was operated on not by Graeme and his team, but by Dr Barrie Scrivener FRACS and Professor William 'Bill' Gibson in Sydney later that same year. The patient, eight-year-old Pia Jeffrey, had some very limited hearing but not enough to effectively understand and learn speech. Her parents weighed up the options and decided for surgery. Graeme followed her progress from Melbourne with great interest. After a two-week recovery period the device was turned on.

Professor Gibson, who had already developed a support group in Sydney for bionic ear recipients, was convinced that the earlier a child could receive an implant and begin learning to process speech, the better for their development. Even Pia, he feared, was older than the ideal age to begin the process. Nevertheless, as time went on, there was no doubt in his mind that Pia was benefiting greatly from the implant. He reported:

> Originally we were lucky to get a single word [from Pia]. Now [after the implant] we are getting three to six strung together in a sentence. Pia is being taught to understand and to be ready to hear something . . . a door slamming, a telephone ringing. Every time you clap your hands that's a sound effect, recognition, remembering, association, the combination of the three. It will accumulate. This is what a baby does. Pia has lost six years and is now starting out on the road with a lot less hearing than a baby has. Nevertheless in five or six years' time she will see the benefits . . . in fact the benefits are obvious now.[72]

Nor was there any doubt in the mind of Pia's mother, Prue, that the implant had been a life-altering success. She relates how she caught Pia playing with the phone, listening to the dial tone. Then the phone rang and 'she was fascinated because she heard her Grandma; she heard a voice on the end of the phone . . . She looked at me and said "Happy birthday!" And when Grandma said, "I love you," loudly and slowly, she got her first message over the phone. That was the day,' recalled Prue, that 'she'd been switched on.'[73]

When the story of the little girl born deaf using the phone and hearing her Grandma say 'I love you' eventually reached the local phone company, they obtained a photo taken of Pia, smiling from ear to ear, and put it on the back cover of the 1992 Sydney telephone directory, which went out to millions of homes and businesses, with the caption: 'Made in Australia—world famous "bionic ear"—the new miracle in sound.'[74] The photo became iconic for the bionic ear story.

For Graeme Clark, the son of a hearing-impaired pharmacist, and former Sydney schoolboy, the photo and caption could hardly have brought more joy and satisfaction. It symbolised everything he had spent his career aiming to achieve.

And the frontiers continued to be pushed back. If brain plasticity was important for being able to gain the most benefit from a cochlear implant, then it seemed only logical that children born deaf should be operated on at a very early age. But there were also concerns. Any surgery brings risks, and Graeme was well aware that one had to be particularly cautious with young children. Also, operating at a very young age gives little time for the child and parents to work with other options, such as sign language or hearing aids, to make the most of any limited hearing capacity.

This dilemma confronted Graeme when he was approached in late 1989 by the parents of two-year-old Sian Neame, who was born profoundly deaf. Sian's parents had begun to suspect something was wrong when at eighteen months of age Sian was still not speaking. Tests confirmed she was deaf. Hearing aids were fitted, and had some limited effect. The parents were confronted with a range of options and often conflicting advice about what to do. Then they heard about the bionic ear project and contacted Graeme Clark. Graeme agreed to review Sian's case. She was very young—years younger than any other child on whom the team had operated. Yet she seemed in all other respects to be an ideal candidate to benefit from an implant. On 30 November 1989, Graeme agreed to do the surgery, which was scheduled for the following year. On 13 March 1990, at two years and six months, Sian became the youngest patient to receive a cochlear implant within Australia.

If Graeme was apprehensive, his fears were soon allayed. Sian recovered quickly from her surgery and was fitted with a receiver. Her parents, Anne and David, reported Sian responding to sounds like footsteps and birds chirping. Soon she was learning to recognise speech and to speak, catching up quickly to children who were born with hearing. Perhaps the most symbolic event, for Sian's parents, was when a few years later her older brothers came complaining to their parents that Sian had been on the phone with her friend from school for half an hour already, and they wanted to use the phone. Her parents broke down in tears. It was the kind of ordinary problem they had not imagined possible only a few years earlier. In fact, Sian was so happy with her bionic ear that she chose eventually to have a double implant, enhancing her hearing capacity even further. She later told Graeme it was the best decision she had ever made.

Just four months after Sian's surgery, the US Food and Drug Administration approved the Australian bionic ear (by this time a twenty-two channel device) as safe and effective for implantation in children between the ages of two and seventeen. The floodgates of worldwide uptake of the bionic ear for young children were about to open. The event was such big news that Graeme and Sian (who was still not yet three) were interviewed on the Channel 10's *Good Morning Australia* television program on 29 July to talk about the use of the bionic ear in children. For anyone seeing young Sian responding

165

and speaking, much like any other child, so soon after the implant surgery, there was little doubt of the device's effectiveness.

Yet while most—including children like Sian, Pia and their parents—were rejoicing that the deaf could now hear, not everyone was happy.

CHAPTER 28

The signing
Deaf community

The process of developing the cochlear implant, and making it commercially viable, was never easy or without opposition. Graeme recalls with some irony and still a sense of surprise that 'when the device started to help children, all hell broke loose with the Deaf community'. For those unfamiliar with the story, this may at first seem surprising. Most, including Graeme, initially assumed that the entire Deaf community would welcome such a breakthrough. So what was the problem?

I chanced to be in Riga, Latvia, in the early 1990s, just a few months after the country, along with the other Baltic states of Estonia and Lithuania, had declared independence from the Soviet Union. They were heady days in the capital. The Latvian friend we were visiting sent my colleague and me out for the day on our own. With proficiency in English, German and Russian, we expected little problem. We were wrong. We had trouble even buying lunch. It seemed that unless we could speak Latvian, no one wanted our money. We knew that everyone spoke Russian. We knew the older folks understood

German, and we knew the younger, university-educated members of the population had a working knowledge of English. Yet they all pretended we had come from a different planet.

When we returned to our friend's tiny student flat hungry and with few souvenirs for our day's effort, we asked her why there was such a fixation with speaking Latvian. She explained patiently that it was difficult for us to understand, as throughout the world there were eighty million native German speakers, one hundred and fifty million Russian speakers, and at least five hundred million native English speakers. There were, however, only about two million native Latvian speakers, whose language and the culture tied to it had been under threat from German, then Russian, and now, with the new open market to the world and tourism, English. They were desperately afraid of losing their native language, and with it, their identity.

What the hearing community often fails to understand is that the various forms of sign language, such as Auslan, which is used in Australia, are not simply a translation of English, or French, or any other spoken language. Each sign language is its own unique language with its own grammar and syntax and its own history and culture built around the community of those who use it as their first language. If you were born deaf in Australia in the 1960s or '70s, for instance, you would likely eventually have been sent to a special school to learn Auslan. You would also have learned to lip-read, but this would become your means of understanding the language of the hearing. Auslan, spoken by only a few thousand people, would become your first language. You could attend Auslan churches, belong to Auslan social groups, and possibly even marry another Auslan speaker. You were not part of a large community, but it was significant and close-knit.

And you did not necessarily see being deaf as a handicap, especially not when you were with other 'native' speakers of Auslan. You felt most comfortable in this community and had no difficulties under-standing or being understood. Now imagine someone comes along and invents a device that means that all children born deaf from that point on will be able to hear and will not need to learn Auslan. But you are too old to easily benefit from the device. And even if you could, it would seem like an admission that being deaf and speaking sign language really was a disability after all. You are suddenly faced with the gradual dying out of what is in effect your native language.

Graeme summarised the situation well when he observed: 'The signing Deaf community had developed a philosophy that deafness was normal, so hearing by any means was a threat to this view. If the implants were successful, their community would be greatly reduced in size, and the community was their world.'[75] In effect, the signing Deaf community felt they were faced with the end of their culture. In retrospect, no one should have been surprised that they did not greet the news of the bionic ear with the same unbridled enthusiasm as the hearing world.

Graeme, with his interest in deafness and the deaf, had already become involved in the Deaf community early in his tenure as a professor in Melbourne. He was aware that there were complex politics within the Deaf community, and great passion connected to them. He recalls the tremendous divide and dispute over the education of deaf children. Some within the community thought deaf children should be taught to lip-read and use any limited hearing they might have. This was known as the auditory/oral group. Another group favoured using signed English along with any residual hearing. They called themselves the total communication group. Finally, there was a very passionate group that advocated teaching Australian sign language. They were known as the Auslan group. Because of Graeme's work in the field he was, at one stage, asked to chair a committee to estab-lish the Deafness Foundation of Victoria, and so inevitably became involved in this debate. What Graeme didn't imagine, however, is that if a 'cure' for deafness were developed, that a debate would erupt about whether or not children should take it up.

It wasn't long before the signing Deaf community became aware that the bionic ear was being offered to children born deaf, and was likely to become the 'default' option chosen by the parents of deaf children. They responded strongly. One Deaf writer in America summarised these sentiments well in a 1986 article titled 'Cochlear implants the final put down':

Hearing people almost always believe that deaf people need to be 'cured' .... A majority culture has no understanding of how deaf people live day by day. It doesn't fit in with their culture. So they try to do something to change it ... Deaf people see the implant as yet another trick foisted off by the medical community to deny us validity as deaf.[76]

Graeme was taken aback. 'In all the years,' he reflected, 'that I had been working at finding a cure for deafness, I never thought to ask the Deaf community if they wanted a cure.' Most of the patients Graeme saw were those who had been hearing, and wanted desperately to have their hearing restored, or the hearing parents of deaf children worried about their future. Graeme Clark, who at every step of his journey had had to learn new skills and new perspectives, once again found himself on a new and unexpected journey of learning.

A significant insight came for Graeme when he read an article by the hearing-impaired journalist Michael Uniacke. The article helped him to understand the perspective of the Deaf community, which he admitted had taken him, and others, largely by surprise. Uniacke had written: 'The signing deaf community views the cochlear implant with anger.' One reason for their anger, according to Uniacke, was 'the bionic ear implies that deaf people are sick', and 'Professor Clark

Graeme receives a cheque from Fred Agar on behalf of the Rotary Club of Melbourne for the first Nerve Deafness Telethon in 1974. Compere Mike Willesee looks on. (Courtesy of Fred and Anna Maria Agar)

A cartoon of Graeme shaking a tin on the streets of Melbourne to raise funds for the Nerve Deafness Telethon in 1974. (Unknown artist)

The team who comprised the first School of Audiology at the Department of Otolaryngology, University of Melbourne, 1974.

Engineers Jim Patrick and Ian Forster display a Mastermos silicon chip designed for the University of Melbourne prototype cochlear implant, 1977. Shrinking this down to something that would fit into an ear stimulator was a major engineering challenge.

Graeme demonstrating with a turban shell how a grass blade passes around the first turn. While fiddling with a shell and a blade of grass on a holiday at Minnamurra Beach in 1977 he realised there was a safe way to insert electrodes into the inner ear.

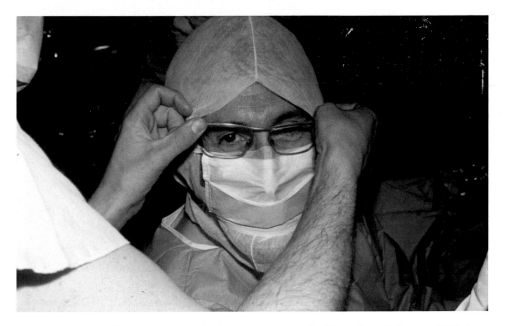

Graeme in surgical gear preparing for his operation on Rod Saunders, 1 August 1978. As he reflected later, his entire career to that point had come down to this one operation.

Graeme and his two youngest patients, Bryn Davey (aged 5) and Scott Smith (aged 10). (Neale Duckworth, *The Age*)

Paul Trainor, the founder of Cochlear, with his wife Marie and Margaret and Graeme at the Clunies Ross medal presentation for excellence in science and technology, Melbourne, 1992. The award recognised that the bionic ear was a partnership between university and industry.

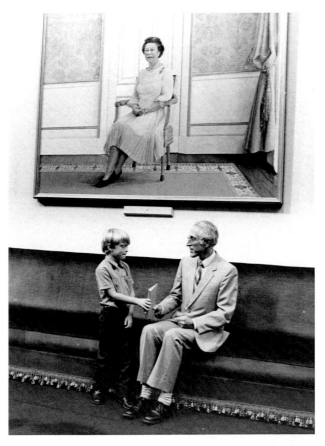

Graeme with son Jonathan and the Advance Australia Award received at Government House, Victoria, in 1986. (Courtesy Advance Australia Award Association)

Graeme with his first adult patient Rod Saunders and young patient Ryan Varasso, in 1998, on the twentieth anniversary of Rod's ground-breaking surgery. (Herald & Weekly Times)

Queen Elizabeth II meets pioneer implant recipients Bryn Davies and Rod Saunders on 23 March 2000 at the Bionic Ear Institute, Melbourne.

Graeme signs the book for fellows of the Royal Society in London in 2004. The book contains signatures of many famous scientists, including that of Sir Isaac Newton. (Courtesy Royal Society London)

Graeme and Margaret with surgeon and implanted children in Taipei, 2003. By now, the implant was being widely used around the world. (Courtesy Taiwan Christian Medical College)

Graeme receiving the Lister Medal from Mr John Black, president of the Royal College of Surgeons, London, in 2010. The Lister Medal is one of the most prestigious prizes in surgical science in the world.

Presentation of the 2013 Lasker–DeBakey award for clinical medical research. The award is one of the highest honours for investigators whose contributions have improved the clinical treatment of patients. From left to right: Dr Goldstein (Chair), Blake Wilson, Ingeborg Hochmair and Graeme Clark.

Graeme Clark at the University of Melbourne's Department of Neural Engineering with his 2015 Fritz J. and Dolores H. Russ Prize, awarded by the US National Academy of Engineering and Ohio University for outstanding achievements in bio-engineering for human welfare. (Peter Casamento/Casamento Photography)

of Richard Dowell, a PhD student being supervised by Graeme, Peter Blamey and Peter Seligman. Graeme was still finding graduate students to be some of his best and most innovative resources. The second significant innovation during this period involved Hugh McDermott and an increase in the number of frequencies extracted from the device, which kept Cochlear Limited ahead of an increasingly competitive field.

Also, Graeme's team (the ARC Human Communication Research Centre), now working out of the University of Melbourne, was able to develop a much improved electrode bundle to be inserted into the inner ear. But all this took funding, and Graeme now had to find a quarter of a million dollars each year to equip and run the university program and the research institute. The success of the Human Communication Research Centre also meant that there was not enough space for the Department of Otolaryngology at the Eye and Ear. In 1990 when the Bionic Ear Institute was moved to Mollison House, on the corner of Albert and Lansdowne streets, Melbourne, this improved the situation significantly. The institute, at Mollison House, has been overseen, from 1992 onwards, by a succession of presidents, including David Brydon, John Calvert-Jones, Michael Robinson and Gerry Moriarty.

The pioneering work of Graeme Clark was destined to have implications beyond the bionic ear. In 2004, while Graeme was still serving as director of the Bionic Ear Institute, he articulated his broader vision for the institute and for bionics.

I'm now collaborating with St Vincent's Hospital and the University of Wollongong to develop intelligent polymers and grow nerves on them, so that we can make better contact with the hearing nerve, and so create better bionic ears. And also, this will allow us, I hope, to take people with broken spinal cords and bridge the gap and allow the nerves to connect from the top to the bottom so that they may be able to feel again, have body function and hopefully walk again . . .

There's tremendous possibilities nowadays for combining medicine and biology with the new advances in technology. And we are getting down to thousandths of a millimetre with nanotechnology. We're developing intelligent plastics. But what we need are people to use this to not only help produce better bionic ears, but also to help people with other neural problems like spinal cord injuries . . . We have expertise—not only with a bionic ear, but with a new field of bionics—which is really biology working closely with electronics and technology. My hope, my desire, is that we'll bring all this together here, in a centre in Australia, to actually have biomedicine, bioengineering. It's much bigger than the bionic ear.[80]

And this dream is continuing to become a reality. With the encouragement gained from the success of Clark's team, and the breakthrough research that lay behind it, researchers at the institute began to work towards a bionic eye, and even neurobionics, which might someday allow those with severed spinal cords to walk again. Through this work and this vision, the Bionic Ear Institute grew into something much broader. After Graeme's retirement as director of the institute in 2006 it was renamed the Bionics Institute, reflecting this wider vision of research in bioengineering.

The Bionics Institute has already been able to support a number of bold projects. In 2012 the institute made international headlines when Dianne Ashworth was implanted with a prototype bionic eye at the Eye and Ear Hospital, helping Australia to catch up to pioneering research in this exciting field taking place in Europe and the United States. When the device, consisting of twenty-four electrodes extending from the back of the eye to a connector behind the ear, was switched on, Dianne was able to detect flashes of light. In a process not unlike what Clark and his team had undertaken in the 1970s and '80s, the team has begun to focus on developing a vision processor that will allow patients to translate these flashes of light into useful images.

Professor Anthony Burkitt, director of Bionic Vision Australia, and Professor Robert Shepherd, head of the Bionics Institute, credited the multidisciplinary approach behind the team's efforts with the result. They also acknowledged the importance of Graeme Clark, whose pioneering work they were continuing to build upon. With the successful implant of the first prototype bionic eye—alongside the continuing advances in the bionic ear coming out of Melbourne—Australia today continues to stand at the forefront of research in bionics. And it all began with one young boy's dream of helping the deaf to hear.

CHAPTER 30

Success and sadness at millennium's turn

As the old century drew to a close and the new millennium beckoned, Graeme, now in his mid-sixties, was able to look back on what had been accomplished. As requests to tell the story of the bionic ear continued to come in, Graeme felt it was time to tell the story more fully from his point of view. With the university's research, the Bionic Ear Institute and Cochlear Limited going well, the girls now out on their own, and son Jonathan in medical school, things were looking very positive on all fronts. Graeme felt he could afford the time to reflect, and to write.

So Graeme set about writing *Sounds from Silence: Graeme Clark and the bionic ear story*. He had kept meticulous records and notes of the many key events and people involved in the success of the bionic ear. Now he had the opportunity to give credit where it was due, to set some records straight, to reveal the amount of opposition and number of hurdles that he and his team had faced, and to reveal something of the man behind the vision. The book appeared in the millennial year, 2000. Allen & Unwin's print run of 10,000 was soon exhausted, and a

Reader's Digest version sold another 40,000 copies. As the author to this point of mostly technical books and scientific articles, Graeme was not accustomed to this large readership. But he should not have been surprised. The telethons had raised the profile of the project in the public arena, and by this time as well, recipients of the implants already numbered in the tens of thousands.

The book gave Graeme a chance to speak freely about the role his personal faith in God had played in helping him remain determined to succeed during the toughest times. He was also able to reveal the importance of family. The book's dedication mentioned the many patients and their families, his colleagues and the many who had made generous donations to the project. But at the very top of the dedication page he thanked Margaret and their five children, his mum and dad, and his sister Robin and brother Bruce.

Back in Camden, Bruce, who was now running their father's chemist shop, was delighted to receive the book. He had always been proud of his big brother. When he finished the book, he took time to write to Graeme to tell him just that, and how much he had meant to him. If Bruce's response appeared emotional, there was a reason for it. He was dying.

Only a few months earlier Graeme had made one of many visits to Camden while in Sydney for work-related meetings. He often took the time to catch the train to Camden and spend a day or two with his father, and with his brother Bruce and his family. On this occasion the brothers decided to play a round of golf on the local course. Graeme soon noticed that Bruce wasn't getting around very well, which was unusual as he had always been very athletic and fit. Bruce explained, somewhat embarrassed, that his bowels had not been moving well and he was feeling some discomfort.

Being a doctor Graeme was immediately concerned and asked if Bruce had been to see anyone about the complaint. He said he had been to see a doctor in Sydney, but had been told there was nothing to it. Graeme was not convinced. When they left the golf course he took Bruce to have a series of X-rays. The results came back inconclusive; but there was enough there, together with Bruce's symptoms, to cause him concern. Perhaps he was worrying too much, but he had always felt part big brother and part second father to Bruce, given their age difference and their closeness. He didn't want to panic Bruce, but he was worried. He arranged for him to see a specialist in Sydney.

Graeme returned to Melbourne to Margaret and his work with the university and the institute, and waited. The phone call from his specialist contact in Sydney who had carried out exploratory surgery confirmed his worst fears. His brother had bowel cancer. Unfortunately secondary tumours had already appeared in the liver. The cancer had spread, and Graeme knew better than most what this meant. He was shattered. He thought of Bruce's wife and their children. And he worried about their father.

Things began to happen very quickly. Close family and friends were contacted with the news. The extended family rallied around Bruce and his family. Further surgery was arranged. A lot of praying was done.

Graeme and Robin had always found their brother Bruce to be courageous and generous. Bruce was adored by Graeme and Margaret's children. He and his family were always there with them for summer holidays at Kiama. He was the one who kept an eye on their parents, and after Dorothy's death in 1987, on their dad back in Camden. He also kept up the family chemist shop. Bruce was at the core of the extended Clark family as well as of his own immediate family.

Bruce made the most of his remaining health and energy. He made a final visit to Graeme and Margaret's home in Eltham for the engagement party of their son Jonathan and his fiancée Marissa who, like Jonathan, was also a medical student. It was a happy occasion, despite the concern everyone had for Bruce. He was again with his extended family for the spectacular Sydney fireworks that saw in the new millennium. And he made one last sojourn with his family to Kiama for the summer holidays. A photo taken on that occasion of the three Clark siblings is still precious to Graeme.

Graeme received a moving last letter from Bruce that still brings tears to his eyes.

Dear Graeme,

I read your letter and was touched by your kind words . . . Despite what . . . others might say about me having a complex about a successful brother I can only say how proud I have been of your achievements and delighted in every way regarding your success . . . I thank you for your prayers and kindness . . . I have really closed shop and have a few good friends around me, but the best is now left to my extended family. I have always enjoyed most my times with my family and with yours and Robin's.

Love Bruce

The end came quickly after that. Graeme remembers watching his father sitting alone at the back of the funeral home while arrangements were beings made, and thinking how very difficult it must be to live to experience the death of your child. He took it, Graeme felt, even harder than he did his wife Dorothy's death more than a decade earlier. It was a sadness that never faded. Only a few months later Colin Clark, aged ninety-six, died.

Graeme, who had only months earlier been looking forward to the new millennium with much anticipation, realised that it was the end of an era. Personal sorrow had cast its shadow on the promise of new beginnings.

CHAPTER 31

'Retirement'

On a recent visit to Graeme's home I was ushered into his office where a microscope was set up on the side of his desk.

'Take a look at this,' he invited.

I put my eye to the microscope and peered inside.

'Do you know what this is?'

'It looks like the cross-section of some sort of bone,' I answered hopefully.

'Not just any bone, it is a cross-section from the bone of the inner ear. Do you see anything else?'

I looked more closely, wondering what it was I might be looking for. Finally I saw it. 'There appears to be a very thin line running across it.'

'Exactly. That's a crack. I always suspected it must be there, but the technology we had at the time wouldn't allow us to detect it.'

'Just what is it I'm looking at?' I finally asked.

'It's a cross-section of Rod Saunders' inner ear bone. It's just come in from the dissection lab. Rod left his body to science so we could study the long-term impact of a cochlear implant on the bone of the inner ear. No one has had an implant longer than Rod. I am writing a paper on the results. That's what's up on the screen.'

'Don't you have younger researchers who could be doing this? I thought you were retired.'

'Well, I like to keep busy and contribute what I can. Besides, Rod was a friend and a good man. I owe him at least this much.'

Retirement, I learned, in the case of a man like Graeme Clark, is a relative concept. In fact, it is hard to apply the concept to Graeme at all. Even as he approaches his eightieth birthday he keeps a busier schedule than many people in their prime. He attends frequent meetings and events, mostly to promote the bionic ear, maintains active contact with the university through an honorary professorship that is more active than honorary, and is still writing and publishing papers. He still actively pursues research towards the next generation of bionic ears through his position of honorary professor of electrical engineering at the University of Melbourne in association with the Centre for Neural Engineering. And, of course, he remains very busy with his children and grandchildren, with nieces and nephews, and with family holidays at Kiama.

Perhaps, rather than retirement, it is better to speak of Graeme's post-Eye and Ear Hospital and post-Bionic Ear Institute career.

As Graeme neared his sixty-fifth birthday, he was approached by the dean of the University of Melbourne Medical School about his retirement from his position as professor of otolaryngology, which he had held since 1970. This took him somewhat by surprise, even though it was not uncommon in the academic world that retirement was expected at sixty-five years of age in order to make way for the next generation of academic leaders. Graeme began to pray about the idea of retirement from his position, but didn't feel any peace about it. He felt there was still much work to do on the further development of the bionic ear. And he still had a lot of energy and enthusiasm for the task.

As university politics played out, a new dean of medicine was appointed and Graeme was once again called in for a meeting. At least this time he knew what to expect, or so he thought. Imagine his surprise when, instead of being encouraged, once more, to consider retirement, he was offered a five-year extension of his contract with a pay rise—along with the new title of laureate professor. Clearly, somewhere along the lines of officialdom, the thinking had changed and the university realised that encouraging one of their most prominent and successful professors of medicine into retirement when he was still actively engaged in groundbreaking research might not be such a good idea.

So Graeme pressed on with his work for another five years, continuing to make significant progress in bionic ear research and to lead the various teams for which he was responsible. At age sixty-nine he felt it was finally time to move on. He retired from all his roles at the university, including laureate professor, head of the Cochlear Implant Program and head of the Cochlear Implant Clinic at the Eye and Ear Hospital.

This left Graeme free to focus all of his attention and energy on the Bionic Ear Institute, which he had founded and served as director of for the past twenty years. One of his first concerns was to secure funding for the position of director so that it did not have to be subsidised through the university. It could also not be assumed that future directors would take on this dual role. An opportunity arose when Graeme received the Prime Minister's Prize for Science in 2004, worth $300,000. He announced that he intended to donate the money to the institute to fund the director's position, but hoped to find ten other donors who would be willing to match his gift. When John Howard, the prime minister at the time, heard what Graeme was doing with his prize, he organised a government grant of six million dollars for the institute. The prime minister held a press conference to make the announcement and also announced that the institute was to be renamed the Graeme Clark Institute in honour of its founder.[81] While this name change never eventuated, Graeme had managed to leave a lasting legacy. With a fully funded director's position, and money to spare for other recurrent running costs, the future of the institute was made much more secure.

By this stage Graeme was now nearing his seventieth birthday and he knew that some in governance of the institute were thinking it was time for new leadership. To make matters more complicated, the Bionic Ear Institute was set up to function in the world of corporate and not university research. So he found, as was a common practice in the corporate world, that he was expected to sign a non-competition clause which meant he could not do work or research for any other group in the field once he left. For a man who still felt he had a lot to offer and didn't feel nearly as old as his birth certificate indicated, this was a difficult pill to swallow. Also, for Graeme, the research had always been about helping the deaf, not about commercial competition. He found this turn of events quite stressful. And once more, he found it the occasion for earnest prayer.

By this time the Graeme Clark Foundation had been founded, through which he was able to direct charitable funding from prizes he received and donations from other sources. On the board of the foundation at the time was Tania Costello, wife of then federal treasurer Peter Costello, and a lawyer. Graeme sought Tania's advice. Fortunately, she was able to persuade him that he did not have to sign such an agreement. So when Graeme at last left his role as founding director of the Bionic Ear Institute in 2006 at seventy-one years of age, he was free to continue to carry out the research he was currently doing and for which grant funding had already been secured.

When La Trobe University learned of the situation they offered Graeme a three-year appointment as the university's first distinguished professor. From 2007 to 2010 Graeme continued his research into advances in bionic ear technology at La Trobe University. Now nearly seventy-five, it seemed to Graeme that perhaps it was finally time to retire. But he still had many projects going and there was so much more he felt he could contribute to advancing bionic ear technology. Even at seventy-five Graeme was still actively publishing academic articles in the field and winning grant money for further research.

At this point he received an interesting and unexpected offer to return to the University of Melbourne, not through the medical school but the school of engineering. Graeme, after a long and distinguished career in surgery and medical research, was appointed honorary professor of electrical engineering. While the position at first seems surprising, it is less so when one considers how much of the research for advances in the bionic ear, and research into bionic spinal cord repair for paraplegia and the bionic eye, was taking place through the field of engineering. For Graeme it was yet another new adventure.

When offered the opportunity to work directly on projects involving bionic eye research, Graeme declined. He chose to continue to concentrate on bionic ear technology, where he felt there was still much progress that could be made. He found the work on the bionic eye exciting, and had worked to encourage this while director of what had now come to be called the Bionics Institute. But he felt that it was best that he continue to focus his career on doing one thing well, and that was the bionic ear. As his eightieth year drew closer, the vision and commitment of the young boy from Camden who wanted to fix ears in order to help deaf people like his father, had not waned.

'Professor Clark, that kiss belongs to you!'

Graeme Clark continues to speak regularly at events promoting the bionic ear. At nearly every venue there is a family or two present with a child who has a cochlear implant, or an adult with a cochlear implant. Invariably they sit at the back and linger afterwards until all the professional colleagues have left. While the content of Graeme's talk may or may not have been of interest, that is of little concern. They have come for one reason: to meet the man who changed their lives. They approach when the auditorium has largely emptied and ask for a quiet word, or maybe a photo taken with Graeme. Although by this point exhausted, Graeme never refuses. He appears, instead, energised by these encounters.

Graeme has received many impressive awards and recognitions, and these usually form an important part of the introduction to the many talks Graeme continues to give. While important, however, these accolades were never a part of Graeme's motivation. When the last photo has been taken and the last family leaves, Graeme is still smiling, though weary. 'That,' says Graeme, 'is the reason I did it.'

Of all the many expressions of thanks he has received over the years from implant recipients and their families, one stands out to him. It was 1990 and he had come under renewed criticism, with the press reporting that some colleagues were still questioning the effectiveness of the device. The grandmother of one young bionic ear recipient read the newspaper article with dismay. She felt compelled to write to Professor Clark, a man she had never met. Of the thousands of letters Graeme has received, this letter remains one of his most memorable.

The grandmother wrote:

Yesterday, in the *Herald*, I read what I felt was unfair, ill-informed, criticism of the cochlear programme . . . I hope this letter reaches you because I wanted so much to thank you for the priceless gift you made possible for our small grandson, Edward. Edward will be three next week, and helping teach him to hear and speak has been pure joy—a miracle that seemed impossible when he lost his hearing following meningitis in May last year . . . Edward received his implant last September and was switched on in October. His reaction was beautiful . . . When the sound came on he dived down behind his father's knee . . . By the end of the session his smile was so wide you could tie it in a bow at the back of his head. He hasn't looked back . . .

That Teddy can distinguish between 'pig' and 'peg', 'house' and 'horse', 'bird' and 'bed', between 's' and 'sh', fills me with unbounded admiration for the man who conceived the operation, and the team behind him, for the technicians who made such fine distinctions possible . . . I have no way to thank you properly, but perhaps Teddy has.

In those early weeks post op he had been aware of sound, but not yet of speech. We were sitting on the sofa having a lesson, practising 'a', when suddenly it came out loud and clear. Then, hardly daring, I said 'i'. He followed, very softly. I went on: 'e', 'o', 'u' and each time Teddy followed. I felt awed, so filled with emotion I couldn't speak. Teddy was shining, as if a light had been switched on. Then, very slowly, he learned over and kissed me gently on the mouth. That kiss belongs to you.[82]

EPILOGUE

APPENDIX 1

Recognitions and awards

Once it became clear that Graeme and his team had accomplished what most thought to be impossible, and had brought the design out of the university laboratory and into the marketplace where tens of thousands could experience the benefits, the recognition and awards from once disbelieving and bemused colleagues began to flow. What is striking about the long list of awards received by Graeme Clark is not only the renown and international prestige of many of them, but their sheer range. Given the many fields Professor Clark had to master in his research into the bionic ear, we find awards covering neuroscience, speech science, surgery, medicine, audiology, acoustics, engineering, biological engineering, business and commerce, political science and even Australian Father of the Year. Some of the more significant awards include:

Honours (civil)
2004   Companion of the Order of Australia (AC)
        (for services to medicine and to science through innovative

research to further the development of cochlear implant tech-nology for worldwide benefit—Australia's highest civil honour)

1983   Officer of the Order of Australia (AO)
(for services to medicine)

Scientific prizes and medals

2015   The Fritz J. and Dolores H. Russ Prize, awarded biennially by the National Academy of Engineering and Ohio University, in recognition of a bioengineering achievement in widespread use that improves the human condition

2013   Lasker–DeBakey Clinical Medical Research Award, awarded by the Lasker Foundation which honours investigators whose contributions have improved the clinical treatment of patients
(one of the most prestigious prizes in science in the world)

2011   CSL Florey Medal, from the Australian Institute of Policy and Science and Commonwealth Serum Laboratories (CSL)
(represents the pinnacle of Australia's biomedical achievements)

2011   Zotterman Medal, awarded by the Nobel Institute for Neurophysiology, Karolinska Institutet, Stockholm
(past recipients have included Lord Edgar Adrian, Nobel prize 1932 and Bert Sakmann, Nobel prize 1991)

2010   Lister Medal, awarded by the Royal College of Surgeons of England and Glasgow, Royal Society, Edinburgh University
(the world's most prestigious award in the surgical sciences; awarded every three years)

2009   Otto Schmitt Award, International Federation of Medical and Biological Engineering
(for exceptional contributions to the advancement of the field of medical and biological engineering; presented every three years)

2007   Zülch Prize from the Gertrud Reemtsma Foundation, administered by Max Planck Society
        (*for exceptional achievement in basic neurological research*)

2007   Lifetime Achievement Award, the Faculty of Medicine, Nursing and Health Sciences, Monash University
        (*the highest award made by the faculty*)

2006   Ian Wark Medal and Lecture, Australian Academy of Science
        (*for contributions to Australian science and industry*)

2005   International Speech Communication Association Medal
        (*for significant contribution to the progress of speech science and technology*)

2005   Royal College of Surgeons of Edinburgh Medal, awarded at the Quincentenary Celebrations of the college
        (*for outstanding contributions to medicine*)

2005   A. Charles Holland Foundation International Prize
        (*for fundamental contribution to the progress of knowledge in the audiological/otological field*)

2005   Excellence in Surgery Award, Royal Australasian College of Surgeons
        (*recognising the highest level of surgical achievement by world standards, advanced innovation in the field, continued quality and worth of the innovation, and the highest standard of ethics*)

2004   Prime Minister's Prize for Science
        (*in recognition of outstanding achievement by Australians in science and technology which promotes human welfare— Australia's premier award in science*)

Academic honours and awards

2013   The Graeme Clark Chair in Audiology and Speech Science, University of Melbourne

2011   The Graeme Clark Research Institute, Tabor College, Adelaide

2009   The Graeme Clark Centre for Innovation in the Sciences, The Scots College, Sydney

2008   The Graeme Clark Foundation

2008   Delivered the inaugural Graeme Clark Oration, held annually at the University of Melbourne

2003   The Graeme Clark Cochlear Scholarship Foundation
(for cochlear implant tertiary students awarded on the basis of academic achievement and commitment to the cochlear ideals of leadership and humanity)

1999–2004   Laureate Professor, University of Melbourne
(for international recognition of scientific achievement)

2002   Aram Glorig Award, International Society of Audiology
(in recognition of a lifetime's contribution to audiology)

2000   Cavalcade of Science Honour Award, Australian Institute of Political Science
(one of the eleven most outstanding Australian scientists of the twentieth century)

1992   Clunies Ross National Science & Technology Award
(for application of science and technology for the benefit of Australia)

1985   Royal Australasian College of Surgeons, John Mitchell Crouch Fellowship Award for Surgical Research
(for an outstanding contribution to fundamental scientific research in surgery)

Fellow or member of academic societies by election

2013   Fellow of the National Academy of Inventors (United States)

2009   Honorary Bragg Membership, Royal Institute of Australia
(one of the initial seventeen outstanding Australian scientists elected)

2007 Fellow of the American Institute of Medical and Biological Engineering

2004 Fellow of the Royal Society
(for contribution to science, both in fundamental research resulting in greater understanding, and in leading and directing scientific and technological progress in industry and research establishments)

2004 Honorary Fellow, Royal College of Surgeons, England
(supreme single award of the college for outstanding achievement in medicine)

2004 Fellow of the Australian Acoustical Society
(for notable contribution to the science and practice of acoustics)

2003 Honorary Fellow, Royal Society of Medicine, London
(for exceptional distinction; recipients drawn from across the world and from a wide range of endeavour, particularly from the medical sciences)

2002 Honorary Member of the American Otological Society
(for longstanding contributions to otology)

1998 Fellow of the Australian Academy of Science
(for outstanding contributions to science)

1998 Fellow of the Australian Academy of Technological Sciences and Engineering
(for outstanding contributions to science and technology)

1992 First Honorary Fellow, Audiological Society of Australia

Honorary doctorates

2013 Honorary Doctor of Health Sciences, University of Technology, Sydney

2010 Doctorate *honoris causa*, University of Zaragoza, Spain

2004 Doctorate of Laws *honoris causa* (Hon. LLD), Monash University, Australia

2003   Doctorate of Engineering (Hon. Deng), Chung Yuan Christian University, Taiwan

2002   Doctorate of Science *honoris causa* (Hon. DSc), University of Wollongong, Australia

1989   Doctorate of Medicine *honoris causa* (Hon. MD), University of Sydney, Australia

1988   Doctorate of Medicine (Hon. MD), Medizinishche Hochschule, Hannover, Germany

APPENDIX 2

Scientific innovations

The bionic ear is not a single, innovative achievement, but the culmination of a number of interrelated innovations and discoveries. In particular, Professor Graeme Clark is credited with the following innovations or discoveries, all of which were vital for the successful development and commercial success of the bionic ear:

- The mapping of the physiological limitations of reproducing the temporal and place coding of sound frequencies with electrical stimulation of the auditory nerves. This research demonstrated that a single-channel stimulation of the auditory nerves would not be able to reproduce the crucial mid-high frequencies of speech.
- The discovery of the method of effectively and safely using multi-channel electrical stimulation of the auditory nerves with an array of electrodes inserted into the cochlea. This discovery is related to Clark's famous turban shell discovery and other studies showing how to effectively and safely insert an electrode bundle into the cochlea.

- The development of an implantable receiver-stimulator, and the discovery of perception of rate, place and intensity of stimulation. Once the first multi-channel prosthesis was implanted, studies of sensations of pitch, timbre and loudness were for the first time able to be carried out.

- The development of a formant-based speech processor for multi-channel electrical stimulation of the auditory central nervous system to give everyday conversational speech understanding to profoundly deaf adults who once had hearing ability. In 1978 Clark discovered that key mid-high frequencies could be of great importance for understanding speech, presented non-simultaneously as electrical stimuli on a place coding basis.

- The perception of complex electrical stimuli and speech features, and acoustic models of electrical stimulation relevant to speech understanding. That is, Clark was able to determine how the brain integrated information along and across multi-channels.

- Improved speech understanding through the transmission of additional speech information along temporal and spatial processing channels, and the general factors responsible for good speech perception.

- The development of bilateral cochlear implants and bimodal hearing. Clark researched and demonstrated the value of twin implants, particularly with reference to the ability to understand speech in the presence of background noise.

- Multi-channel vocoder and fixed filter electrical stimulation of the auditory central nervous system of children born deaf which showed the importance of early exposure for place pitch perception. This allowed Clark and his team to discover the neural plasticity of speech components and develop effective speech perception and production.

Professor Clark's pioneering research also created several new sub-disciplines of study. These include:

- The physiology of the electrical stimulation of the auditory nervous system.
- The psychophysics of electrical stimulation of the auditory system.
- The application of speech science to a sensory prosthesis.
- The histophathology of ear implants and electrical stimulation of the auditory nerve.
- Implant surgery of the inner ear.

Patents held jointly by Graeme Clark

1977   Hearing Prosthesis—Improvements in Prothesis.
        G. Clark, J. Patrick, I. Forster, Y. Tong, R. Black.

1978   Hearing Prosthesis—Improved Electrode Array.
        G. Clark, J. Patrick, Q. Bailey.

1979   Hearing Prosthesis—Speech Processor.
        G. Clark, J. Patrick, J. Millar, P. Seligman, Y. Tong.

1979   Improvements to Speech Processor.
        G. Clark, J. Patrick, J. Millar, P. Seligman, Y. Tong.

1982   Hearing Prosthesis—Receiver/Stimulator.
        H. McDermott, P. Blamey, R. Black, G. Clark, D. Money, J. Patrick, Y. Tong.

1985   Hearing Prosthesis—Prosthetic 'Flippy Tip' Electrode Array.
        G. Clark and H. Franz.

1990   Hearing Prosthesis—Bimodal Speech Processor.
        P. Blamey, G. Dooley, G. Clark, P. Seligman.

1992   Curved 22-Channel Intracochlear Electrode Array.
        S. Xu, J. Xu, H. Seldon, F. Neilson, G. Clark, R. Shepherd.

1994   Cochlear Implant System for Residual Hearing Stimulation.
        A. Vandali, G. Clark.

1994 Transient Emphasis Speech Processing.
   A. Vandali, G. Clark.

1994 Multiple Pulse Per Period (MP3) Electrical Stimulation Strategy for Cochlear Implants.
   L. Irlicht, G. Clark.

1995 Cochlear Implant Devices.
   G. Clark, L. Cohen, P. Bushby.

2001 A Travelling Wave Sound Processor.
   P. Blamey, H. McDermott, B. Swanson, J. Patrick, G. Clark.

APPENDIX 3

Selected publications

During the course of his scientific career Graeme Clark authored or co-authored over four hundred articles in refereed scientific journals along with numerous reviews, book chapters and monographs. The following is a small representation of his published contribution to topics relevant to the development of cochlear implants.

Books and selected book chapters

Clark G.M., *Cochlear Implants: Fundamentals and applications*, New York: Springer-Verlag, 2003

Clark G.M., 'Cochlear implants', in S. Greenberg (ed.), *Springer Handbook of Auditory Research: Speech processing in the auditory system*, New York: Springer-Verlag, 2003

Clark G.M., 'Learning to understand speech with the cochlear implant', in M. Fahle & T. Poggiio (eds), *Perceptual Learning*, Cambridge: MIT Press, 2002, pp. 147–60

Clark G.M., 'Cochlear Implants: Historical perspectives', in Geoff Plant & Karl-Erik Spens (eds), *Profound Deafness and Speech Communication*, London: Whur Publishers, 1995

Clark G.M., in collaboration with Blamey P.J., Brown A.M., Busby P.A., Dowell R.C., Franz B.K.-H.G., Pyman B.C., Shepherd R.K., Tong Y.C., Webb R.L., Hirshorn M.S., Kuzma J.A., Mecklenburg D.J., Money D.K., Patrick J.F. & Seligman P.M., *Nucleus Multi-electrode Cochlear Implant* (*Advances in Oto-Rhino-Laryngology*; Vol. 38), Basel: Karger, 1987

Clark G.M., Black, R.C., Forster, I.C., Patrick, J.F. & Tong, Y.C., 'Design criteria of a multiple-electrode cochlear implant hearing prosthesis', in H. Levitt, J.M. Pickett & R. Houde (eds), *Sensory Aids for the Hearing Impaired*, IEEE Press, New York, 1980, pp. 457–9

Selected refereed scientific papers

Clark G.M., 'The multi-channel cochlear implant: Multi-disciplinary development of electrical stimulation of the cochlea and the resulting clinical benefit', *Hearing Research* (Lasker Award), 2015, vol. 322, pp. 4–13

Clark G.M., 'The multichannel cochlear implant for severe-to-profound hearing loss', *Nature Medicine*, 2013, vol. 19, no. 10, pp. 1236–9

Clark G.M., Clark J.C., Furness J.B., 'The evolving science of cochlear implants', *Journal of the American Medical Association*, 2013, vol. 310, no. 12, pp. 1225–6

Clark G.M., 'The multi-channel cochlear implant and the relief of severe-to-profound deafness', *Cochlear Implants International*, 2012, vol. 13, no. 2, pp. 69–85

Clark G.M., 'Personal reflections on the multi-channel cochlear implant and a view of the future', *Journal of Rehabilitation Research and Development*, 2008, vol. 45, no. 5, pp. 651–94

Wei B., Clark G., O'Leary S., Shepherd R.K. & Robins-Browne R., 'Meningitis after cochlear implantation', *British Medical Journal*, 2007, vol. 335, pp. 1058

Clark G.M., 'The multiple-channel cochlear implant: The interface between sound and the central nervous system for hearing, speech, and language in deaf people: A personal perspective', *Philosophical Transactions of the Royal Society*, 2006, vol. 361, pp. 791–810

Chen B.K., Clark G.M. & Jones R., 'Evaluation of trajectories and contact pressures for the straight nucleus cochlear implant electrode array: A two-dimensional application of finite element analysis', *Medical Engineering and Physics*, 2003, vol. 2, pp. 141–7

SELECTED PUBLICATIONS

Surowiecki V.N., Sarant J.Z., Maruff P., Blamey P.J., Busby P.A. & Clark G.M., 'Cognitive processing in children using cochlear implants: The relationship between visual memory, attention and executive functions and developing language skills', *Annals of Otology, Rhinology and Laryngology*, 2002, vol. 111, pp. 119–26

Cohen L.T., Saunders E. & Clark G.M., 'Psychophysics of a prototype peri-modiolar cochlear implant electrode array', *Hearing Research*, 2001, vol. 155, pp. 63–81

Busby P.A. & Clark G.M., 'Pitch estimation by early-deafened subjects using a multiple-electrode cochlear implant', *Journal of the Acoustical Society of America*, 2000, vol. 107, pp. 547–58

Pyman B., Blamey P., Lacy P., Clark G. & Dowell R., 'The development of speech perception in children using cochlear implants: Effects of etiologic factors and delayed milestones', *American Journal of Otology*, 2000, vol. 21, pp. 57–61

Vandali A.E., Whitford L.A., Plant K.L. & Clark G.M., 'Speech perception as a function of electrical stimulation rate: Using the Nucleus 24 cochlear implant system', *Ear and Hearing*, 2000, vol. 21, pp. 608–24

van Hoesel R.J.M. & Clark G.M., 'Speech results with a bilateral multi-channel cochlear implant subject for spatially separated signal and noise', *Australian Journal of Audiology*, 1999, vol. 21, pp. 23–8

Flynn M.C., Dowell R.C. & Clark G.M., 'Aided speech recognition abilities of adults with a severe hearing loss', *Journal of Speech and Hearing Research*, 1998, vol. 41, pp. 285–99

Busby P.A. & Clark G.M., 'Pitch and loudness estimation for single and multiple pulse per period electric pulse rates by cochlear implant patients', *Journal of the Acoustical Society of America*, 1997, vol. 101, pp. 1687–95

van Hoesel R.J.M. & Clark G.M., 'Psychophysical studies with two binaural cochlear implant subjects', *Journal of the Acoustical Society of America*, 1997, vol. 102, pp. 495–507

Blamey P.J., Dooley G.J., Parisi E.S. & Clark G.M., 'Pitch comparisons of acoustically and electrically evoked auditory sensations', *Hearing Research*, 1996, vol. 99, pp. 139–50

McKay C.M., McDermott H.J. & Clark G.M., 'The perceptual dimensions of single-electrode and non-simultaneous dual-electrode stimuli in cochlear implantees', *Journal of the Acoustical Society of America*, 1996, vol. 99, pp. 1079–90 van Hoesel R.J.M. & Clark G.M., 'Fusion and laterization study with two binaural cochlear implant patients', *Annals of Otology, Rhinology and Laryngology*, 1995, vol. 104 (suppl. 166), pp. 233–5

Dahm M., Clark G.M., Franz B.K.-H.G., Shepherd R.K. & Burton M.J., 'Cochlear implantation in children: labyrinthitis following pneumococcal otitis media in unimplanted and implanted cat cochleas', *Acta Oto-Laryngologica*, 1994, vol. 114, pp. 620–5

McKay C.M., McDermott H.J. & Clark G.M., 'Pitch percepts associated with amplitude-modulated current pulse trains in cochlear implantees', *Journal of the Acoustical Society of America*, 1994, vol. 96, pp. 2664–73

Busby P.A., Tong Y.C. & Clark G.M., 'The perception of temporal modulations by cochlear implant patients', *Journal of the Acoustical Society of America*, 1993, vol. 97, pp. 124–31

Dahm M., Shepherd R.K. & Clark G.M., 'The postnatal growth of the temporal bone and its implications for cochlear implantation in children', *Acta Oto-Laryngologica*, 1993, (suppl. 505), pp. 5–39

van Hoesel R., Tong Y.C., Hollow R.D. & Clark G.M., 'Psychophysical and speech perception studies: A case report on a binaural cochlear implant subject', *Journal of the Acoustical Society of America*, 1993, vol. 94, pp. 3178–89

Busby P.A., Tong Y.C. & Clark G.M., 'Psychophysical studies using a multiple-electrode cochlear implant in patients who were deafened early in life', *Audiology*, 1992, vol. 31, pp. 95–111

Clark G.M., Shepherd R.K., Franz B.K.-H.G., Dowell R.C., Tong Y.C., Blamey P.J., Webb R.L., Pyman B.C., McNaughton J., Bloom D., Kakulas B.A. & Siejka S., 'The histopathology of the human temporal bone and auditory central nervous system following cochlear implantation in a patient: Correlation with psychophysics and speech perception results', *Acta Oto-Laryngologica*, 1988, (suppl. 448), pp. 1–65

Clark G.M., Busby P.A., Roberts S.A., Dowell R.C., Tong Y.C., Blamey P.J., Nienhuys T.G.W., Mecklenburg D.J., Webb R.L., Pyman B.C. & Franz B.K.-H.G., 'Preliminary results for the Cochlear Corporation multi-electrode intracochlear implants on six prelingually deaf patients', *American Journal of Otology*, 1987, vol. 8, pp. 234–9

Clark G.M., Blamey P.J., Busby P.A., Dowell R.C., Franz B.K.-H.G., Musgrave G.N., Nienhuys T.G.W., Pyman B.C., Roberts S.A., Tong Y.C., Webb R.L.,

SELECTED PUBLICATIONS

Kuzma J.A., Money D.K., Patrick J.F. & Seligman P.M., 'A multiple-electrode intracochlear implant for children', *Archives of Otolaryngology*, 1987, vol. 113, pp. 825–8

Tong Y.C. & Clark G.M., 'Loudness summation, masking, and temporal interaction for sensations by electric stimulation of two sites in the human cochlea', *Journal of the Acoustical Society of America*, 1986, vol. 79, pp. 1958–66

Shepherd R.K., Clark G.M., Pyman B.C. & Webb R.L., 'Banded intracochlear electrode array: Evaluation of insertion trauma in human temporal bones', *Annals of Otology, Rhinology and Laryngology*, 1985, vol. 94, pp. 55–9

Clark G.M., Tong Y.C. & Dowell R.C., 'Comparison of two cochlear implant speech-processing strategies', *Annals of Otology, Rhinology and Laryngology*, 1984, vol. 93, pp. 127–31

Clark G.M., Tong Y.C., Patrick J.F., Seligman P.M., Crosby P.A., Kuzma J.A. & Money D.K., 'A multi-channel hearing prosthesis for profound-to-total hearing loss', *Journal of Medical Engineering and Technology*, 1984, vol. 8, pp. 3–8

Clark G.M., Tong Y.C. & Dowell R.C., 'Clinical results with a multi-channel pseudobipolar system', *Annals of the New York Academy of Sciences*, 1983, vol. 405, pp. 370–7

Clark G.M., Crosby P.A., Dowell R.C., Kuzma J.A., Money D.K., Patrick J.F., Seligman P.M. & Tong Y.C., 'The preliminary clinical trial of a multi-channel cochlear implant hearing prosthesis', *Journal of the Acoustical Society of America*, 1983, vol. 74, pp. 1911–14

Tong Y.C., Clark G.M., Blamey P.J., Busby P.A. & Dowell R.C., 'Psychophysical studies for two multiple-channel cochlear implant patients', *Journal of the Acoustical Society of America*, 1982, vol. 71, pp. 153–60

Clark G.M., Tong Y.C. & Martin L.F., 'A multiple-channel cochlear implant. An evaluation using closed-set spondaic words', *Journal of Laryngology and Otology*, 1981, vol. 95, pp. 461–4

Clark G.M., Tong Y.C., Martin L.F. & Busby P.A., 'A multiple-channel cochlear implant. An evaluation using an open-set word test', *Acta Oto-Laryngologica*, 1981, vol. 91, pp. 173–5

Clark G.M., Tong Y.C., Martin L.F.A., Busby P.A., Dowell R.C., Seldon H.L. & Patrick J.F., 'A multiple-channel cochlear implant: An evaluation using nonsense syllables', *Annals of Otology, Rhinology and Laryngology*, 1981, vol. 90, pp. 227–30

Tong Y.C., Clark G.M., Seligman P.M. & Patrick J.F., 'Speech processing for a multiple-electrode cochlear implant hearing prosthesis', *Journal of the Acoustical Society of America*, 1980, vol. 68, pp. 1897–9

Clark G.M., Patrick J.F. & Bailey Q.R., 'A cochlear implant round window electrode array', *Journal of Laryngology and Otology*, 1979, vol. 93, pp. 107–9

Clark G.M., Pyman B.C. & Bailey Q.R., 'The surgery for multiple-electrode cochlear implantations', *Journal of Laryngology and Otology*, 1979, vol. 93, pp. 215–23

Clark G.M., Black R.C., Forster I.C., Patrick J.F. & Tong Y.C., 'Design criteria of a multiple-electrode cochlear implant hearing prosthesis', *Journal of the Acoustical Society of America*, 1978, vol. 63, pp. 631–3

Clark G.M., Tong Y.C., Black R.C., Forster I.C., Patrick J.F. & Dewhurst D.J., 'A multiple electrode cochlear implant', *Journal of Laryngology and Otology*, 1977, vol. 91, pp. 935–45

Clark G.M. & Hallworth R.J., 'A multiple-electrode array for a cochlear implant', *Journal of Laryngology and Otology*, 1976, vol. 90, pp. 623–7

Clark G.M., Hallworth R.J. & Zdanius K., 'A cochlear implant electrode', *Journal of Laryngology and Otology*, 1975, vol. 89, pp. 787–92

Clark G.M., 'A hearing prosthesis for severe perceptive deafness—experimental studies', *Journal of Laryngology and Otology*, 1973, vol. 87, no. 10, pp. 929–45

Clark G.M., Kranz H.G. & Minas H., 'Behavioral thresholds in the cat to frequency modulated sound and electrical stimulation of the auditory nerve', *Experimental Neurology*, 1973, vol. 41, pp. 190–200

Clark G.M., 'Responses of cells in the superior olivary complex of the cat to electrical stimulation of the auditory nerve', *Experimental Neurology*, 1969, vol. 24, no. 1, pp. 124–36

ACKNOWLEDGEMENTS

This biography would not have been possible without the assistance of very many people. First of all, the cooperation and encouragement of Graeme Clark and his wife Margaret were invaluable at several levels. They allowed me into their home and their lives, and gave generous access to a range of material needed for the writing of this biography. Also, I am much indebted to Gordon and Marilyn Darling for their generous financial support of this project via a gift to the Graeme Clark Research Institute of Tabor College, Adelaide, which has assisted with the editing and publication of the work. I would also like to thank Claire Bell, whose careful readings of the manuscript have removed many imperfections. The members of my writers' group, the Literati, were also kind enough to give one of their meetings over to a review of an early version of the manuscript. Their suggestions have resulted in many improvements. Jim Patrick, from Cochlear Limited, also read the manuscript and made many helpful suggestions.

Finally, I would like to thank Elizabeth Weiss, Angela Handley, Meaghan Amor and the rest of the team at Allen & Unwin for being willing to take on this project and for the many suggestions which have helped shape its final form.

I also need to acknowledge the wealth of information at my disposal as I approached this project. The development of the bionic ear has been one of the best documented advances of modern Australian medical science. Graeme himself has spoken and written numerous times on his work developing the bionic ear. The most thorough source, also containing a short account of his life, was published by Allen & Unwin in 2000 as *Sounds from Silence: Graeme Clark and the bionic ear story*. It is a rich first-person narrative of the development of the bionic ear, and contains a number of diagrams as well as medical and technical detail. Also, in his series of six Boyle Lectures in 2007, published by ABC Books as *Restoring the Senses*, Graeme covered some of this same material, though in a less technical way. The story of the bionic ear itself and some of the early recipients was told by June Epstein in her 1989 book *The Story of the Bionic Ear* (Hyland House). A very comprehensive account of the origins and growth of Cochlear Limited written by Veronica Bondarew and Peter Seligman has recently appeared as *The Cochlear Story* (CSIRO, 2012). A number of DVDs have also been produced about Graeme Clark and the bionic ear. The most recent of these, *Never Say Never: The Graeme Clark story*, by Paul and Margaret Drane (Pipeline Media, 2013) is particularly well done. These volumes and other sources have been most useful and have made the task of writing a biography of Graeme Clark much easier in many ways. Between them, they document the story of the bionic ear and its development in much detail.

But the present volume is not so much the story of the bionic ear as it is the story of the life of the man whose vision made it a reality. I have necessarily been briefer in the accounts of the technological advancements, surgeries and commercial development of the cochlear implant than many of these sources, focusing instead on the life of Graeme Clark before, after and in the midst of these momentous achievements.

NOTES

1   Graeme Clark, *Sounds from Silence: Graeme Clark and the bionic ear story*, Allen & Unwin, Sydney, 2000, p. 112f.

2   Graeme Clark, unpublished autobiographical notes, 1997.

3   Otolaryngology derives from the Greek and means literally 'the study of the ears and throat'. Otolaryngologists are commonly referred to as ENTs, or Ear, Nose and Throat specialists, even though the word for 'nose' is not ordinarily included in the composite word. When it is, the speciality is called otorhinolaryngology, but this is generally thought to be too long and hard to pronounce, so the shorter term is more common.

4   Cf. Paul and Margaret Drane, *Never Say Never: The Graeme Clark story*, DVD, Pipeline Media, 2013.

5   A PhD thesis was even done on class structure in Camden during that period by Jack Mason; Graeme's family was given a copy for their help and interest in his study.

6   Clark, *Sounds from Silence*, p. 24.

7   Clark, *Sounds from Silence*, p. 22.

8   Cf. H. Levitt, 'Digital hearing aids: Wheelbarrows to ear inserts', *ASHA Leader*, vol. 12, no. 17, 2007: 28–30; and Mara Mills, 'Hearing aids and the history of electronics miniaturization', *IEEE Annals of the History of Computing*, vol. 33, no. 2, 2011: 24–45.

9   Clark, *Sounds from Silence*, p. 27.

10   Clark, *Sounds from Silence*, p. 29.

11   Clark, *Sounds from Silence*, p. 32.

12   Clark, *Sounds from Silence*, p. 34.

13   Basil Hetzel, *Chance and Commitment: Memoirs of a medical scientist*, Wakefield Press, Adelaide, 2005, pp. 27, 30.

14   Renate Howe, *A Century of Influence: The Australian Student Christian Movement 1896–1996*, University of NSW Press, Sydney, 2009.

15   See Hetzel, *Chance and Commitment*, p. 29.

16   Tabor Adelaide graduation address, March 2012.

17   From Margaret's speech on the occasion of Graeme's 75th birthday celebrations, 16 September 2010.

18   Clark, *Sounds from Silence*, p. 37.

19   Clark, *Sounds from Silence*, p. 39.

20   Graeme Clark, 'Wilberforce, Christianity and the workplace', unpublished lecture, 2007.

21   Cf. Tabor Adelaide graduation address, March 2012.

22   For this and the following quote, Graeme Clark, unpublished autobiographical notes, January 1997.

23   Clark, unpublished autobiographical notes.

24   From a transcribed conversation between Peter Howson, Ken Howson and Graeme Clark discussing the establishment of the chair of otolaryngology, n.d.

25   Included in Clark, *Sounds from Silence*, p. 72.

26   Clark, 'Wilberforce, Christianity and the workplace'.

27   Clark, *Sounds from Silence*, p. 74.

28   Cited in Graeme Clark, 'Cochlear Implants: Historical perspectives', in Geoff Plant and Karl-Erik Spens (eds), *Profound Deafness and Speech Communication*, Whur Publishers, London, 1995, p. 169.

29   Cited in June Epstein, *The Story of the Bionic Ear*, Hyland House, Melbourne, 1989, p. 34.

30   Clark, 'Cochlear Implants: Historical perspectives', pp. 165ff. Similar experiments were later carried out on the electrical stimulation of sound in 1855 by Duchenne of Boulogne and Rudolf Brenner in 1868.

31   Cf. G. Gersuni and A. Volokhov, 'On the effect of alternating currents on the cochlea', *The Journal of Physiology*, vol. 89, no. 2, 1937: 113–21. Significantly, they determined through the use of 'single-condenser discharges and

induction shocks' that 'the sensations which originated during the flow of such [alternating] currents through the ear are of a tonal nature and closely resemble in their character those arising from sound stimulation of the same frequency': p. 113.

32 Veronica Bondarew and Peter Seligman, *The Cochlear Story*, CSIRO publishing, Melbourne, 2012, pp. 25f.

33 Bondarew and Seligman, *The Cochlear Story*, p. 26.

34 Clark, *Sounds from Silence*, p. 44.

35 Clark, *Sounds from Silence*, p. 61 and Clark, unpublished autobiographical notes.

36 Bondarew and Seligman, *The Cochlear Story*, p. 29.

37 Bondarew and Seligman, *The Cochlear Story*, p. 29.

38 Conversation with Peter Howson, Ken Howson and Graeme Clark.

39 Bondarew and Seligman, *The Cochlear Story*, p. 29.

40 Reported in Clark, *Sounds from Silence*, p. 133.

41 Singer's views on this matter surprised many of his readers, but were made clear in the various comments on the use of animals for experimentation when no other alternative could be found and a significant human benefit was likely in the second edition of his classic work, *Animal Liberation*, New York: HarperCollins, 1990, especially pp. 31–3, 45–8, 61–5, 90–2.

42 For the complete list compiled by Graeme, see Clark, *Sounds from Silence*, Appendix 3.

43 Cf. Bondarew and Seligman, *The Cochlear Story*, p. 30f.

44 This short film and other similar material can be found at the National Film & Sound Archives of Australia.

45 Clark, *Sounds from Silence*, p. 85.

46 Clark, *Sounds from Silence*, p. 86.

47 Interview with George Negus, broadcast on *George Negus Tonight*, 27 May 2004.

48 Clark, *Sounds from Silence*, p. 65.

49 Clark, *Science and God: Reconciling science with the Christian faith*, Anzea Books, Melbourne, 1979, p. 44.

50 For MacKay's views on this question see D. M. Mackay, 'The Bankruptcy of Determinism,' in *The New Scientist*, 1970.

51 Bondarew and Seligman, *The Cochlear Story*, p. 27.

52 Bondarew and Seligman, *The Cochlear Story*, p. 28.

53 Cited in Bondarew and Seligman, *The Cochlear Story*, p. 29.

54   Letter dated 24 August 2007.

55   Clark, *Sounds from Silence*, p. 125.

56   Clark, *Sounds from Silence*, p. 127.

57   Clark, *Sounds from Silence*, p. 133.

58   Graeme Clark, 'Guided Evolution', an unpublished press release, August 2012.

59   Clark, 'Guided evolution'.

60   Clark, 'Guided evolution'.

61   Clark, *Sounds from Silence*, p. 213f.

62   Clark, *Sounds from Silence*, p. 144.

63   Graeme Clark, 'Foreword', in Bondarew and Seligman, *The Cochlear Story*, p. v.

64   Graeme Clark, *Cochlear Implants: Fundamentals and applications*, Springer-Verlag, New York, 2003.

65   Cited in 'Cochlear celebrates 30 years of hearing revolution', <www.cochlear.com /wps/wcm/connect/au/about/cochlear-30-anniversary>.

66   Letter dated 22 August 2007.

67   Bondarew and Seligman, *The Cochlear Story*, p. 2.

68   Bondarew and Seligman, *The Cochlear Story*, p. 2.

69   Clark, *Sounds from Silence*, p. 166.

70   See Epstein, *The Story of the Bionic Ear*, p. 74f.

71   Philip McIntosh, 'Bionic ear lets boys hear again', *Age*, 11 June 1986.

72   Cited in Epstein, p. 83f.

73   Epstein, p. 84.

74   Clark, *Sounds from Silence*, p. 178.

75   Graeme Clark, *Restoring the Senses*, ABC Books, Sydney, 2007, p. 71.

76   *The Disability Rag* (February 1986, no author), cited in Clark, *Restoring the Senses*, p. 72.

77   Cited in Clark, *Sounds from Silence*, p. 171f.

78   Clark, *Restoring the Senses*, p. 73.

79   Interview with George Negus, *George Negus Tonight*, 27 May 2004.

80   Interview with George Negus, *George Negus Tonight*, 27 May 2004.

81   Melinda Rout, '$5.7m birthday gift sounds good', *Herald Sun*, 2 April 2005.

82   Cited in Clark, *Sounds from Silence*, p. 181f.

INDEX

INDEX